FOR LANCELOT ANDREWES

ESSAYS ON STYLE AND ORDER

FOR LANCELOT ANDREWES

ESSAYS ON STYLE AND ORDER

BY

T. S. ELIOT

*'Thou, Lord, Who walkest in the midst
of the golden candlesticks, remove not, we
pray Thee, our candlestick out its place;
but set in order the things which are want-
ing among us, and strengthen those which
remain, and are ready to die.'*

LONDON

Faber & Gwyer

FIRST PUBLISHED IN MCMXXVIII
BY FABER & GWYER LIMITED
24 RUSSELL SQUARE, LONDON, W.C.I
PRINTED IN GREAT BRITAIN
BY BUTLER & TANNER LIMITED
FROME AND LONDON
ALL RIGHTS RESERVED

FOR MY MOTHER

PREFACE

HAD I wished to publish a volume of collected literary essays, this book would have been much bigger. The reader may be puzzled to know why I selected these articles and in this order. I wished to indicate certain lines of development, and to disassociate myself from certain conclusions which have been drawn from my volume of essays, *The Sacred Wood*. To make my present position clear I have three small books in preparation which will not be ready for a considerable time. Meanwhile, I have made bold to unite these occasional essays merely as an indication of what may be expected, and to refute any accusation of playing 'possum. The general point of view may be described as classicist in literature, royalist in politics, and anglo-catholic in religion. I am quite aware that the first term is completely vague, and easily lends itself to clap-trap; I am aware that the second term is at present without definition, and easily lends itself to what is almost worse than clap-trap, I mean temperate conservatism; the third term does not rest with me to define. The uncommon reader who is interested by these scattered papers may possibly be interested by the small volumes which I have in preparation: *The School of Donne*; *The Outline of Royalism*; and *The Principles of Modern Heresy*.

I wish to acknowledge my obligation to the editors of *The Times Literary Supplement*, *Theology*, *The Dial* (New York), and *The Forum* (New York), in which reviews these essays appeared.

T. S. E.

CONTENTS

I   LANCELOT ANDREWES   PAGE 13

II   JOHN BRAMHALL   33

III   NICCOLO MACHIAVELLI   49

IV   FRANCIS HERBERT BRADLEY   67

V   BAUDELAIRE IN OUR TIME   86

VI   THOMAS MIDDLETON   100

VII   A NOTE ON RICHARD CRASHAW   117

VIII   THE HUMANISM OF IRVING BABBITT   126

[xi]

I

LANCELOT ANDREWES

THE Right Reverend Father in God, Lancelot Bishop of Winchester, died on September 25, 1626. During his lifetime he enjoyed a distinguished reputation for the excellence of his sermons, for the conduct of his diocese, for his ability in controversy displayed against Cardinal Bellarmine, and for the decorum and devotion of his private life. Some years after Andrewes's death Lord Clarendon, in his *History of the Rebellion*, expressed regret that Andrewes had not been chosen instead of Abbott to the Archbishopric of Canterbury, for thus affairs in England might have taken a different course. By authorities on the history of the English Church Andrewes is still accorded a high, perhaps the highest, place; among persons interested in devotion his 'Private Prayers' are not unknown. But

[13]

among those persons who read sermons, if they read them at all, as specimens of English prose, Andrewes is little known. His sermons are too well built to be readily quotable; they stick too closely to the point to be entertaining. Yet they rank with the finest English prose of their time, of any time. Before attempting to remove the remains of his reputation to a last resting place in the dreary cemetery of literature, it is desirable to remind the reader of Andrewes's position in history.

The Church of England is the creation not of the reign of Henry VIII or of the reign of Edward VI, but of the reign of Elizabeth. The *via media* which is the spirit of Anglicanism was the spirit of Elizabeth in all things; the last of the humble Welsh family of Tudor was the first and most complete incarnation of English policy. The taste or sensibility of Elizabeth, developed by her intuitive knowledge of the right policy for the hour and her ability to choose the right men to carry out that policy, determined the future of the English Church. In its persistence in finding a mean between Papacy and Presbytery the English Church under Elizabeth became something representative of the finest spirit of England of the time. It came to reflect not only the personality of Elizabeth herself, but the best community of her subjects of every rank. Other religious impulses, of varying degrees of spiritual value, were to assert themselves with greater vehemence during the next two reigns. But the Church at the end of the reign of Elizabeth, and as developed in certain directions under the next reign, was a masterpiece of ecclesiastical statesmanship. The same authority that made use of Gresham, and of Walsingham, and of Cecil, appointed Parker to the Archbishopric of Canterbury; the same authority was later to appoint Whitgift to the same office.

To the ordinary cultivated student of civilization the genesis of a Church is of little interest, and at all events we must not confound the history of a Church with its spiritual meaning. To the ordinary observer the English Church in history means Hooker and Jeremy Taylor —and should mean Andrewes also: it means George Herbert, and it means the churches of Christopher Wren. This is not an error: a Church is to be judged by its intellectual fruits,

by its influence on the sensibility of the most
sensitive and on the intellect of the most
intelligent, and it must be made real to the
eye by monuments of artistic merit. The
English Church has no literary monument
equal to that of Dante, no intellectual monument equal to that of St. Thomas, no devotional
monument equal to that of St. John of the
Cross, no building so beautiful as the Cathedral
of Modena or the basilica of St. Zeno in
Verona. But there are those for whom the
City churches are as precious as any of the
four hundred odd churches in Rome which are
in no danger of demolition, and for whom St.
Paul's, in comparison with St. Peter's, is not
lacking in decency; and the English devotional
verse of the seventeenth century—admitting
the one difficult case of conversion, that of
Crashaw—finer than that of any other country
or religion at the time.

The intellectual achievement and the prose
style of Hooker and Andrewes came to complete the structure of the English Church as
the philosophy of the thirteenth century crowns
the Catholic Church. To make this statement
is not to compare the 'Laws of Ecclesiastical

Polity' with the 'Summa'. The seventeenth century was not an age in which the Churches occupied themselves with metaphysics, and none of the writings of the fathers of the English Church belongs to the category of speculative philosophy. But the achievement of Hooker and Andrewes was to make the English Church more worthy of intellectual assent. No religion can survive the judgment of history unless the best minds of its time have collaborated in its construction; if the Church of Elizabeth is worthy of the age of Shakespeare and Jonson, that is because of the work of Hooker and Andrewes.

The writings of both Hooker and Andrewes illustrate that determination to stick to essentials, that awareness of the needs of the time, the desire for clarity and precision on matters of importance, and the indifference to matters indifferent, which was the general policy of Elizabeth. These characteristics are illustrated in the definition of the Church in the second book of the 'Ecclesiastical Polity'. ('The Church of Christ which was from the beginning is and continueth until the end.') And in both Hooker and Andrewes—the latter

the friend and intimate of Isaac Casaubon—
we find also that breadth of culture, an ease
with humanism and Renaissance learning,
which helped to put them on terms of equality
with their Continental antagonists and to
elevate their Church above the position of a
local heretical sect. They were fathers of a
national Church and they were Europeans.
Compare a sermon of Andrewes with a sermon
by another earlier master, Latimer. It is not
merely that Andrewes knew Greek, or that
Latimer was addressing a far less cultivated
public, or that the sermons of Andrewes are
peppered with allusion and quotation. It is
rather that Latimer, the preacher of Henry
VIII and Edward VI, is merely a Protestant;
but the voice of Andrewes is the voice of a
man who has a formed visible Church behind
him, who speaks with the old authority and the
new culture. It is the difference of negative
and positive: Andrewes is the first great
preacher of the English Catholic Church.

The sermons of Andrewes are not easy reading. They are only for the reader who can
elevate himself to the subject. The most
conspicuous qualities of the style are three:

[18]

ordonnance, or arrangement and structure, precision in the use of words, and relevant intensity. The last remains to be defined. All of them are best elucidated by comparison with a prose which is much more widely known, but to which I believe that we must assign a lower place—that of Donne. Donne's sermons, or fragments from Donne's sermons, are certainly known to hundreds who have hardly heard of Andrewes; and they are known precisely for the reasons because of which they are inferior to those of Andrewes. In the introduction to an admirable selection of passages from Donne's sermons, which was published a few years ago by the Oxford Press, Mr. Logan Pearsall Smith, after 'trying to explain Donne's sermons and account for them in a satisfactory manner', observes:

And yet in these, as in his poems, there remains something baffling and enigmatic which still eludes our last analysis. Reading these old hortatory and dogmatic pages, the thought suggests itself that Donne is often saying something else, something poignant and personal, and yet, in the end, incommunicable to us.

We may cavil at the word 'incommunicable', and pause to ask whether the incommunicable is not often the vague and unformed; but the statement is essentially right. About Donne there hangs the shadow of the impure motive; and impure motives lend their aid to a facile success. He is a little of the religious spell-binder, the Reverend Billy Sunday of his time, the flesh-creeper, the sorcerer of emotional orgy. We emphasize this aspect to the point of the grotesque. Donne had a trained mind; but without belittling the intensity or the profundity of his experience, we can suggest that this experience was not perfectly controlled, and that he lacked spiritual discipline.

But Bishop Andrewes is one of the community of the born spiritual, one

che in questo mondo,
contemplando, gustò di quella pace.

Intellect and sensibility were in harmony; and hence arise the particular qualities of his style. Those who would prove this harmony would do well to examine, before proceeding to the sermons, the volume of *Preces Privatæ*. This book, composed by him for his private devotions, was printed only after his death; a few manuscript copies may have been given away during his lifetime—one bears the name of William Laud. It appears to have been written in Latin and translated by him into Greek; some of it is in Hebrew; it has been several times translated into English. The most recent edition is the translation of F. E. Brightman, with an interesting introduction, in 1903 (Methuen). They are almost wholly an arrangement of Biblical texts, and of texts from elsewhere in Andrewes's immense theological reading. Canon Brightman has a paragraph of admirable criticism of these prayers which deserves to be quoted in full:

But the structure is not merely an external scheme or framework: the internal structure is as close as the external. Andrewes develops an idea he has in his mind: every line tells and adds something. He does not expatiate, but moves forward: if he repeats, it is because the repetition has a real force of expression; if he accumulates, each new word or phrase represents a new development, a substantive addition to what he is saying. He assimilates his material and advances by means of it. His quotation is not decoration or irrelevance, but the matter in which he expresses what he wants to say. His single thoughts are no doubt often suggested by the words he borrows, but the thoughts are made his own, and the constructive force, the fire that fuses them, is his own. And this internal, progressive, often poetic structure is marked outwardly. The editions have not always reproduced this feature of the *Preces*, nor perhaps

is it possible in any ordinary page to represent the structure
adequately; but in the manuscript the intention is clear
enough. The prayers are arranged, not merely in paragraphs, but in lines advanced and recessed, so as in a measure
to mark the inner structure and the steps and stages of the
movement. Both in form and in matter Andrewes's prayers
may often be described rather as hymns.

The first part of this excellent piece of criticism may be applied equally well to the prose
of Andrewes's sermons. The prayers themselves, which, as Canon Brightman seems to
hint, should take for Anglicans a place beside
the Exercises of St. Ignatius and the works of
St. François de Sales, illustrate the devotion
to private prayer (Andrewes is said to have
passed nearly five hours a day in prayer) and
to public ritual which Andrewes bequeathed
to William Laud; and his passion for order in
religion is reflected in his passion for order in
prose.

Readers who hesitate before the five large
volumes of Andrewes's sermons in *The Library
of Anglo-Catholic Theology* may find their introduction more easy through the *Seventeen Sermons on the Nativity*, which were published
separately in a small volume by Griffith, Far-
ran, Okeden and Welsh, in *The Ancient and*

Modern Library of Theological Literature, and which can still be picked up here and there. It is an additional advantage that these sermons are all on the same subject, the Incarnation; they are the Christmas Day sermons preached before King James between 1605 and 1624. And in the sermons preached before King James, himself a theologian, Andrewes was not hampered as he sometimes was in addressing more popular audiences. His erudition had full play, and his erudition is essential to his originality.

Bishop Andrewes, as was hinted above, tried to confine himself in his sermons to the elucidation of what he considered essential in dogma; he said himself that in sixteen years he had never alluded to the question of pre-destination, to which the Puritans, following their Continental brethren, attached so much importance. The Incarnation was to him an essential dogma, and we are able to compare seventeen developments of the same idea. Reading Andrewes on such a theme is like listening to a great Hellenist expounding a text of the 'Posterior Analytics': altering the punctuation, inserting or removing a comma

[23]

or a semi-colon to make an obscure passage
suddenly luminous, dwelling on a single word,
comparing its use in its nearer and in its
most remote contexts, purifying a disturbed
or cryptic lecture-note into lucid profundity.
To persons whose minds are habituated to feed
on the vague jargon of our time, when we have
a vocabulary for everything and exact ideas
about nothing—when a word half-understood,
torn from its place in some alien or half-
formed science, as of psychology, conceals
from both writer and reader the utter meaning-
lessness of a statement, when all dogma is in
doubt except the dogmas of sciences of which
we have read in the newspapers, when the language of theology itself, under the influence
of an undisciplined mysticism of popular
philosophy, tends to become a language of
tergiversation—Andrewes may seem pedantic
and verbal. It is only when we have saturated
ourselves in his prose, followed the movement
of his thought, that we find his examination of
words terminating in the ecstasy of assent.
Andrewes takes a word and derives the world
from it; squeezing and squeezing the word
until it yields a full juice of meaning which

we should never have supposed any word to
possess. In this process the qualities which
we have mentioned, of ordonnance and precision, are exercised.

Take, almost at random, a passage from
Andrewes's exposition of the text 'That there
is born unto you this day a Saviour, Which is
Christ the Lord, in the City of David' (Luke
ii. 10, 11). Any passage that we can choose
must be torn violently from its context.

Who is it? Three things are said of this Child by the
Angel. (1) He is 'a Saviour'. (2) 'Which is Christ.' (3)
'Christ the Lord.' Three of his titles, well and orderly
inferred one of another by good consequence. We cannot
miss one of them; they be necessary all. Our method on
earth is to begin with great; in heaven they begin with good
first.

First, then, 'a Saviour'; that is His name, Jesus, *Soter*; and
in that Name His benefit, *Salus*, 'saving health or salvation'.
Such a name as the great Orator himself saith of it, *Soter, hoc
quantum est? Ita magnum est ut latino uno verbo exprimi non
possit*. 'This name Saviour is so great as no one word can
express the force of it.'

But we are not so much to regard the *ecce* how great it is,
as *gaudium* what joy is in it; that is the point we are to speak
to. And for that, men may talk what they will, but sure
there is no joy in the world to the joy of a man saved; no joy
so great, no news so welcome, as to one ready to perish, in
case of a lost man, to hear of one that will save him. In

[25]

danger of perishing by sickness, to hear of one will make him
well again; by sentence of the law, of one with a pardon to
save his life; by enemies, of one that will rescue and set him
in safety.   Tell any of these, assure them but of a Saviour, it
is the best news he ever heard in his life.   There is joy in the
name of a Saviour.   And even this way, this Child is a
Saviour too.   *Potest hoc facere, sed hoc non est opus Ejus.*
'This He can do, but this is not His work'; a farther matter
there is, a greater salvation He came for.   And it may be we
need not any of these; we are not presently sick, in no fear of
the law, in no danger of enemies.   And it may be, if we
were, we fancy to ourselves to be relieved some other way.
But that which He came for, that saving we need all; and
none but He can help us to it.   We have therefore all cause
to be glad for the Birth of this Saviour.

And then, after this succession of short sentences—no one is more master of the short
sentence than Andrewes—in which the effort
is to find the exact meaning and make that
meaning live, he slightly but sufficiently alters
the rhythm in proceeding more at large:

I know not how, but when we hear of saving or mention
of a Saviour, presently our mind is carried to the saving of
our skin, of our temporal state, of our bodily life, and farther
saving we think not of.   But there is another life not to be
forgotten, and greater the dangers, and the destruction more
to be feared than of this here, and it would be well sometimes
we were remembered of it.   Besides our skin and flesh a
soul we have, and it is our better part by far, that also hath
need of a Saviour; that hath her destruction out of which, that

hath her destroyer from which she would be saved, and those would be thought on. Indeed our chief thought and care would be for that; how to escape the wrath, how to be saved from the destruction to come, whither our sins will certainly bring us. Sin it is will destroy us all.

In this extraordinary prose, which appears to repeat, to stand still, but is nevertheless proceeding in the most deliberate and orderly manner, there are often flashing phrases which never desert the memory. In an age of adventure and experiment in language, Andrewes is one of the most resourceful of authors in his devices for seizing the attention and impressing the memory. Phrases such as 'Christ is no wild-cat. What talk ye of twelve days?' or 'the word within a word, unable to speak a word', do not desert us; nor do the sentences in which, before extracting all the spiritual meaning of a text, Andrewes forces a concrete presence upon us.

Of the wise men come from the East:

It was no summer progress. A cold coming they had of it at this time of the year, just the worst time of the year to take a journey, and specially a long journey in. The ways deep, the weather sharp, the days short, the sun farthest off, *in solstitio brumali,* 'the very dead of winter'.

Of 'the Word made flesh', again:

I add yet farther; what flesh? The flesh of an infant. What, *Verbum infans*, the Word an infant? The Word, and not be able to speak a word? How evil agreeth this! This He put up. How born, how entertained? In a stately palace, cradle of ivory, robes of estate? No; but a stable for His palace, a manger for His cradle, poor clouts for His array.

He will not hesitate to hammer, to inflect, even to play upon a word for the sake of driving home its meaning:

Let us then make this so accepted a time in itself twice acceptable by our accepting, which He will acceptably take at our hands.

We can now better estimate what is this that we have called relevant intensity, for we have had enough of passages from Andrewes to recognize the extremity of his difference from Donne.

Everyone knows a passage from a sermon of Donne's, which is given by Mr. Pearsall Smith under the title of 'I am Not all Here'.

I am here speaking to you, and yet I consider by the way, in the same instant, what it is likely you will say to one another, when I have done, you are not all here neither; you are here now, hearing me, and yet you are thinking that you have heard a better sermon somewhere else of this text before; you are here, and yet you think you could have heard some other doctrine of downright *Predestination* and *Reprobation* roundly delivered somewhere else with more edification to you; you are here, and you remember yourselves that now yee think of it: This had been the fittest time, now, when everybody else is at church, to have made such and such a private visit; and because you would bee there, you are there,

after which Mr. Pearsall Smith very happily places the paragraph on 'Imperfect Prayers':

A memory of yesterday's pleasures, a feare of to-morrow's dangers, a straw under my knee, a noise in mine eare, a light in mine eye, an anything a nothing, a fancy, a Chimera in my braine, troubles me in my prayer. So certainly is there nothing, nothing in spirituall things, perfect in this world.

These are thoughts which would never have come to Andrewes. When Andrewes begins his sermon, from beginning to end you are sure that he is wholly in his subject, unaware of anything else, that his emotion grows as he penetrates more deeply into his subject, that he is finally 'alone with the Alone', with the mystery which he is seeking to grasp more and more firmly. One is reminded of the words of Arnold about the preaching of Newman. Andrewes's emotion is purely contemplative; it is not personal, it is wholly evoked by the object of contemplation, to which it is adequate;

his emotion is wholly contained in and explained by its object. But with Donne there is always the something else, the 'baffling' of which Mr. Pearsall Smith speaks in his introduction. Donne is a 'personality' in a sense in which Andrewes is not: his sermons, one feels, are a 'means of self-expression'. He is constantly finding an object which shall be adequate to his feelings; Andrewes is wholly absorbed in the object and therefore responds with the adequate emotion. Andrewes has the *goût pour la vie spirituelle*, which is not native to Donne. On the other hand, it would be a great mistake to remember only that Donne was called to the priesthood by King James against his will, and that he accepted a benefice because he had no other way of making a living. Donne had a genuine taste both for theology and for religious emotion; but he belonged to that class of persons, of which there are always one or two examples in the modern world, who seek refuge in religion from the tumults of a strong emotional temperament which can find no complete satisfaction elsewhere. He is not wholly without kinship to Huysmans.

But Donne is not the less valuable, though

he is the more dangerous for this reason. Of the two men, it may be said that Andrewes is the more medieval, because he is the more pure, and because his bond was with the Church, with tradition. His intellect was satisfied by theology and his sensibility by prayer and liturgy. Donne is the more modern —if we are careful to take this word exactly, without any implication of value, or any suggestion that we must have more sympathy with Donne than with Andrewes. Donne is much less the mystic; he is primarily interested in man. He is much less traditional. In his thought Donne has, on the one hand, much more in common with the Jesuits, and, on the other hand, much more in common with the Calvinists, than has Andrewes. Donne many times betrays the consequences of early Jesuit influence and of his later studies in Jesuit literature; in his cunning knowledge of the weaknesses of the human heart, his understanding of human sin, his skill in coaxing and persuading the attention of the variable human mind to Divine objects, and in a kind of smiling tolerance among his menaces of damnation. He is dangerous only for those who find

[31]

in his sermons an indulgence of their sensibility, or for those who, fascinated by 'personality' in the romantic sense of the word
—for those who find in 'personality' an ulti-
mate value—forget that in the spiritual hierarchy there are places higher than that of
Donne. Donne will certainly have always
more readers than Andrewes, for the reason
that his sermons can be read in detached
passages and for the reason that they can be
read by those who have no interest in the
subject. He has many means of appeal, and
appeals to many temperaments and minds,
and, among others, to those capable of a certain wantonness of the spirit. Andrewes will
never have many readers in any one generation, and his will never be the immortality of
anthologies. Yet his prose is not inferior to
that of any sermons in the language, unless it
be some of Newman's. And even the larger
public which does not read him may do well
to remember his greatness in history—a place
second to none in the history of the formation
of the English Church.

II

JOHN BRAMHALL[1]

JOHN BRAMHALL, Bishop of Derry under
Charles I and Primate of Ireland under
Charles II, is not at all an easy subject for a
biography. He was a great man; but either
by defect of genius or by ill-luck he is not
known as he should be known, and his works
are not read as they should be read. Indeed,
it is largely ill luck. Not only were his immense
energy and ability divided among a number
of important actions, so that he has never
become the symbolical representative of anything; but some of his most important activity
was exerted upon causes which are now forgotten. As Bishop of Derry, as the lieutenant
of Wentworth and Laud, he did much to
reform and establish the Irish Church and

[1] *Archbishop Bramhall.* By W. J. Sparrow-Simpson,
D.D. (In the English Theologians Series.) S.P.C.K.

[33]   c

to bring it into conformity with the English Church; he saw his work largely undone by Cromwell; as Primate of Ireland during the first years of Charles II, and in his old age, he set to work to build it up again. Had his labours been in England instead of Ireland he might now be better remembered. His middle years were spent in exile; and perhaps it is the work he performed during these years, often in illness, danger, and vicissitudes, that should earn him particular gratitude from his Church. This is a chapter of Church history which is too little known; few people realize how near in those times the English Church came to perishing utterly, or realize that had the Commonwealth survived a few years longer the Church would have fallen into a disorder from which it might never have recovered. During the exile Bramhall was the stoutest inheritor of the tradition of Andrewes and Laud.

Dr. Sparrow-Simpson has treated the history of Bramhall's career in Ireland and his activities abroad during the Commonwealth fully, but with a proper sense of proportion. He leaves himself space to devote several chapters to Bramhall's controversial writings; he is specially to be praised for the skill with which he has digested these writings and condensed and organized so much various information into two hundred and fifty-one pages. With the purely historical matter I am not competent to deal; Bramhall's life includes an important part of the history of the Church and the history of England. But there is still much interest to be found in Bramhall's writings, and some of them are very much to the point at the present day. One part of his work that is of particular importance is his controversy with Hobbes. It is sometimes cited by historians of philosophy, but has never received the attention it deserves. Bramhall, as Dr. Sparrow-Simpson points out, had by no means the worst of the argument, and the whole debate, with the two striking and opposed personalities engaged in it, throws light upon the condition of philosophy and theology at that time. The most important of the questions at issue are two: the freedom of the will and the relation between Church and State.

Thomas Hobbes was one of those extraordinary little upstarts whom the chaotic motions of the Renaissance tossed into an eminence which they hardly deserved and have never lost. When I say the Renaissance I mean for this purpose the period between the decay of scholastic philosophy and the rise of modern science. The thirteenth century had the gift of philosophy, or reason; the later seventeenth century had the gift of mathematics, or science; but the period between had ceased to be rational without having learned to be scientific. There was nothing particularly new about the determinism of Hobbes; but he gave to his determinism and theory of sense perception a new point and piquancy by applying it, so to speak, almost to topical questions; and by his metaphor of Leviathan he provided an ingenious framework on which there was some peg or other to hang every question of philosophy, psychology, government, and economics.

Hobbes shows considerable ingenuity and determination in his attempt to carry out his theory of the Will rigorously to explain the whole and every aspect of human behaviour. It is certain that in the end he lands himself in sophistries. But at the time of Hobbes and Bramhall, and indeed ever since until recently, it was impossible that a controversy on this subject should keep to the point. For a philosopher like Hobbes has already a mixed attitude, partly philosophic and partly scientific; the philosophy being in decay and the science immature. Hobbes's philosophy is not so much a philosophy as it is an adumbration of the universe of material atoms regulated by laws of motion which formed the scientific view of the world from Newton to Einstein. Hence there is quite naturally no place in Hobbes's universe for the human will; what he failed to see is that there was no place in it for consciousness either, or for human beings. So his only philosophical theory is a theory of sense perception, and his psychology leaves no place in the world for his theory of government. His theory of government has no philosophic basis: it is merely a collection of discrete opinions, prejudices, and genuine reflections upon experience which are given a spurious unity by a shadowy metaphysic.

The attitude of Hobbes toward moral philosophy has by no means disappeared from human thought; nor has the confusion between moral philosophy and a mechanistic psychology. There is a modern theory, closely akin to that of Hobbes, which would make value reside entirely in the degree of organization of natural impulses. I cite the following passage from an important book by one of the most acute of younger psychologists:

Anything is valuable which will satisfy an appetency without involving the frustration of some equal or more important appetency; in other words, the only reason which can be given for not satisfying a desire is that more important desires will thereby be thwarted. Thus morals become purely prudential, and ethical codes merely the expression of the most general schemes of expediency to which an individual or a race has attained.[1]

And Mr. Bertrand Russell, in his book, *What I Believe*, p. 43, sings the same tune:

The practical need of morals arises from the conflict of desires, whether of different people or of the same person at different times or even at one time. A man desires to drink, and also to be fit for his work next morning. We think him immoral if he adopts the course which gives him the smaller total satisfaction of desire.

The difficulty with such theories [2] is that

[1] Richards, *Principles of Literary Criticism*, p. 48.
[2] A thoroughgoing 'Behaviourism', as of Professor Watson, is a different affair.

[38]

they merely remove the inherently valuable a
further degree; just as Hobbes's Theory of
Will removes freedom from the individual
considered as the object of psychology, but
really implies the reality of freewill in society.
It will be remembered that Hobbes wished to
maintain the activity of human legislation in
his deterministic universe; so he considered
that law acts as a deterrent force. He did not
consider that if human laws themselves are
created by the same necessity under which
human beings act when encouraged or deterred
by the laws, then the whole system ceases to
have any meaning, and all values, including
his own value of good government, disappear.

It is not to be expected that the arguments
advanced by Bramhall against this position
should appear very powerful when opposed to
the reasonings of modern disciples of Hobbes.
But in their own time and place they were
excellent. I disregard that part of Bramhall's
reasoning which consists in showing that
Hobbes's system was incompatible with Christianity. Hobbes was here in a very weak
position of which the Bishop with praiseworthy
slyness took full advantage. Hobbes was

undoubtedly an atheist and could hardly have
been unconscious of the fact; but he was no
Spinoza, and would hardly have been willing
to sacrifice his worldly prospects for the sake
of establishing consistency in his argument.
Therefore he has always the worst of the debate. But this is a minor point. Bramhall
was able to meet Hobbes also on his own
ground. His method of attack illustrates very
clearly his type of mind. It was not a subtle
mind: it had not the refinement necessary
to make a scholastic metaphysician, nor was it
the mind of a doctor of the Church who could
develop and explicate the meaning of a dogma.
It was essentially common sense and right
instinct, a mind not gifted to discover truth
but tenacious to hold it. It was typical of
the best theological minds of that age. Hobbes
suffers from not only a tactical but a real
disadvantage in his confusion of the spheres
of psychology and ethics. Bramhall is single-
minded; he does not penetrate the real philosophical incoherence of Hobbes's position; but
he touches the point of practical importance
and implies the profounder objection to Hobbes
when he says simply that Hobbes makes

praise and blame meaningless. 'If a man be born blind or with one eye, we do not blame him for it; but if a man have lost his sight by his intemperance, we blame him justly.' This objection is finally unanswerable.

I have asserted that Hobbes's psychological analysis of the human mind has no rational connection with his theory of the State. But it has, of course, an emotional connection; one can say that both doctrines belong naturally to the same temperament. Materialistic determinism and absolutist government fit into the same scheme of life. And this theory of the State shows the same lack of balance which is a general characteristic of philosophers after the Renaissance. Hobbes merely exaggerates one aspect of the good State. In doing so he developed a particularly lamentable theory of the relation between Church and State.

There is no question to which a man like Hobbes can give a less satisfactory answer than that of Church and State. For Hobbes thought in extremes, and in this problem the extreme is always wrong. In the relation of Church and State, a doctrine when pushed to the extreme may even be transformed to the opposite of itself. Hobbes has something in common with Suarez.

Bramhall's position on this subject is characteristic of his sense of realities and his ability to grasp what was expedient. He had also what Hobbes lacked, the historical sense, which is a gift not only of the historian, but of the efficient lawyer, statesman, or theologian. His account of the relations of the English kings with the Papacy, from the earliest times, and his selection of parallels from the history of continental Europe, show both wide knowledge and great skill in argument. His thinking is a perfect example of the pursuit of the *via media*, and the *via media* is of all ways the most difficult to follow. It requires discipline and self-control, it requires both imagination and hold on reality. In a period of debility like our own, few men have the energy to follow the middle way in government; for lazy or tired minds there is only extremity or apathy: dictatorship or communism, with enthusiasm or with indifference. An able Conservative writer, Mr. Keith Feiling, in his *England under the Tudors and*

Stewarts, refers to Hobbes as 'the acutest thinker of the age'. It would be equally true to say that he is the most eminent example in his age of a particularly lazy type of thinker. At any rate, the age owes a very great part of its distinction, both in England and in France, to thinkers of wholly the opposite type to Hobbes.

The French Church in the time of Louis XIV ('*il fut gallicain, ce siècle, et janseniste*') resembled the English Church under the Stuarts in several respects. In both countries a strong and autocratic civil Government controlled and worked with a strongly national Church. In each country there was a certain balance of power; in France between the throne and the papacy; in England an internal balance of power between strong personalities. There was much in common between Bramhall and Bossuet. But between Bramhall and Hobbes there is no sympathy whatever. Superficially their theories of the kingship bear some resemblance to each other. Both men were violently hostile to democracy in any form or degree. Both men believed that the monarch should have absolute power.

Bramhall affirmed the divine right of kings: Hobbes rejected this noble faith, and asserted in effect the divine right of power, however come by. But Bramhall's view is not so absurdly romantic, or Hobbes's so soundly reasonable, as might seem. To Bramhall the king himself was a kind of symbol, and his assertion of divine right was a way of laying upon the king a double responsibility. It meant that the king had not merely a civil but a religious obligation toward his people. And the kingship of Bramhall is less absolute than the kingship of Hobbes. For Hobbes the Church was merely a department of the State, to be run exactly as the king thought best. Bramhall does not tell us clearly what would be the duties of a private citizen if the king should violate or overturn the Christian religion, but he obviously leaves a wide expedient margin for resistance or justified rebellion. It is curious that the system of Hobbes, as Dr. Sparrow-Simpson has observed, not only insists on autocracy but tolerates *unjustified* revolution. Hobbes's theory is in some ways very near to that of Machiavelli, with this important exception, that he has none of

Machiavelli's profound observation and none of Machiavelli's limiting wisdom. The sole test and justification for Hobbes is in the end merely material success. For Hobbes all standards of good and evil are frankly relative.

It is extraordinary that a philosophy so essentially revolutionary as that of Hobbes, and so similar to that of contemporary Russia, should ever have been supposed to give any support to Toryism. But its ambiguity is largely responsible for its success. Hobbes was a revolutionary in thought and a timid conservative in action; and his theory of government is congenial to that type of person who is conservative from prudence but revolutionary in his dreams. This type of person is not altogether uncommon. In Hobbes there are symptoms of the same mentality as Nietzsche: his belief in violence is a confession of weakness. Hobbes's violence is of a type that often appeals to gentle people. His specious effect of unity between a very simple theory of sense perception and an equally simple theory of government is of a kind that will always be popular because it appears to be intellectual but is really emotional, and therefore very soothing to lazy minds.

Bramhall's abilities of thought and language are nowhere better displayed than in his *Just Vindication of the English Church*. As for the language of Bramhall, I think that Dr. Sparrow-Simpson does him less than justice. It is true that he employs in his vocabulary the most extraordinary confections of Latinity, but the catalogue of some of these expressions which Dr. Sparrow-Simpson gives would lead one to believe that they occur in every sentence. And although Bramhall is not an easy writer, his phrases are lucid and direct and occasionally have real beauty and rhythm. A theologian of his powers, at that period of English prose, a man trained on the theology and the style of Bishop Andrewes, could hardly fail to write prose of distinction.

Every sudden passionate heat or misunderstanding or shaking of charity amongst Christians, though it were even between the principal pastors of the Church, is not presently schism. As that between Saint Paul and Barnabas in the Acts of the Apostles—who dare say that either of them were schismatic? or that between Saint Hierome and Ruffinus, who charged one another mutually with heresy; or that between Saint Chrysostom and Epiphanius, who refused to join in prayers; Saint Chrysostom wishing that Epiphanius might never return home alive, and Epiphanius wishing that Saint Chrysostom might not die a Bishop; both which things, by the just disposition of Almighty God, fell out according to the passionate and uncharitable desires of these holy persons; who had Christian charity still radicated in their hearts, though the violent torrent of sudden passion did for a time beat down all other respects before it.

This is rather heavy going, and the word 'radicated' is one of those blemishes to which Dr. Sparrow-Simpson calls attention; but the style has distinction. In prose style, as well as in theology, Bramhall is a link between the generation of Andrewes and the generation of Jeremy Taylor. The prose of Bramhall is great prose only in the sense that it is good prose of a great epoch. I cannot believe that Bramhall was a great preacher. Andrewes and Donne and Taylor had a poetic sensibility; that is to say, they had the sensitiveness necessary to record and to bring to convergence on a theological point a multitude of fleeting but universal feelings. Their words linger and echo in the mind as Bramhall's never do; we forget Bramhall's phrases the moment we turn away from Bramhall's subject.

But for *ordonnance*, logical arrangement, for

mastery of every fact relevant to a thesis, Bramhall is surpassed only by Hooker; and I am not sure that in the structure of the *Just Vindication of the English Church* he does not surpass even Hooker. And this book is no antiquity; it is a work which ought to be studied by anyone to whom the relation of Church and State is an actual and importunate problem. There could hardly be a greater difference than that between the situation during the first half of the seventeenth century and the situation to-day. Yet the differences are such as to make the work of Bramhall the more pertinent to our problems. For they are differences in relation to a fundamental unity of thought between Bramhall, and what he represents, and ourselves.

III

NICCOLO MACHIAVELLI

'BECAUSE this is to be asserted in general of men, that they are ungrateful, fickle, false, cowards, covetous, and as long as you succeed they are yours entirely.' This sentence, and similar sentences torn from their context, have rankled and worried the minds of men for four hundred years: the words of a retired, inoffensive, quiet Florentine patriot occupied in chopping trees and conversing with peasants on his meagre estate. Machiavelli has been the torment of Jesuits and Calvinists, the idol of Napoleons and Nietzsches, a stock figure for Elizabethan drama, and the exemplar of a Mussolini or a Lenin. Machiavelli has been called a cynic; but there could be no stronger inspiration to 'cynicism' than the history of Machiavelli's reputation. No history could illustrate better than that of the reputation of Machiavelli the triviality and the irrelevance of influence. His message has been falsified by persistent romanticism ever since his death. To the humbug of every century Machiavelli has contributed. And yet no great man has been so completely misunderstood. He is always placed a little askew. He does not belong with Aristotle, or with Dante, in political theory; he attempted something different. He does not belong with Napoleon, and still less with Nietzsche. His statements lend themselves to any modern theory of the State, but they belong with none.

On the occasion of Niccolo Machiavelli's anniversary, we should concern ourselves not so much with the history of his influence—which is merely the history of the various ways in which he has been misunderstood—as with the nature of his thought and the reasons why it should have had such influence.

'So that in the first place I put for a general inclination of all mankind a perpetual and restless desire of power after power, that ceaseth only in death.' Such words of Hobbes seem at first to be uttered in the same tone as those quoted from Machiavelli; and the two names

[50]

have often been brought together; but the spirit and purpose of Hobbes and of Machiavelli are wholly different. *The Prince* is often taken in the same sense as *Leviathan*. But Machiavelli is not only not a philosopher of politics in the sense of Aristotle and Dante, he is still less a philosopher in the sense of Hobbes. He has the lucidity of Aristotle and the patriotism of Dante, but with Hobbes he has little in common. Machiavelli is wholly *devoted*—to his task of his own place and time; yet by surrendering himself to the cause of his particular State, and to the greater cause of the united Italy which he desired, he arrives at a far greater impersonality and detachment than Hobbes. Hobbes is not passionately moved by the spectacle of national disaster; he is interested in his own theory; and we can see his theory as partly an outcome of the weaknesses and distortions of his own temperament. In the statements of Hobbes about human nature there is often an over-emphasis, a touch of spleen arising probably from some perception of the weakness and failure of his own life and character. This over-emphasis, so common in a certain type of philosopher since

Hobbes's time, may be rightly associated with cynicism. For true cynicism is a fault of the temperament of the observer, not a conclusion arising naturally out of the contemplation of the object; it is quite the reverse of 'facing facts'. In Machiavelli there is no cynicism whatever. No spot of the weaknesses and failures of his own life and character mars the clear glass of his vision. In detail, no doubt, where the meanings of words suffer a slight alteration, we feel a conscious irony; but his total view was unimpaired by any such emotional colour. Such a view of life as Machiavelli's implies a state of the soul which may be called a state of innocence. A view like Hobbes's is slightly theatrical and almost sentimental. The impersonality and innocence of Machiavelli is so rare that it may well be the clue to both his perpetual influence over men and the perpetual distortion which he suffers in the minds of men less pure than himself.

We do not mean that Machiavelli is wholly cold and impassive. On the contrary, he provides one more piece of evidence that great intellectual power arises from great passions. Machiavelli was not only a patriot, but his

[52]

patriotic passion is the motor of his mind. It is all very well for writers like Lord Morley to present Machiavelli as a stealthy inhuman surgeon, indifferent to moral exhortation and caring only for his clinical examination. Lord Morley had not, like Machiavelli, seen his country torn and ravaged, humiliated not only by foreign invaders, but by foreign invaders brought in by factious native princes. The humiliation of Italy was to Machiavelli a personal humiliation, and the origin of his thought and his writing.

This intense nationalism by no means suppressed or distorted in Machiavelli the other moral or spiritual values. Only, he is in his writings occupied with these from one point of view always, occupied with them always in their relation to the State. His conception of the State is a large and generous one. He is the adviser of the Prince only because he cares passionately for the good of the commonwealth. For a man like Napoleon—who himself spoke highly of Machiavelli, and whose sense of reality made Machiavelli very sympathetic to him—Machiavelli could have felt only aversion; a foreign usurper and a violent

egotist Napoleon would have seemed to him.
And Machiavelli is not interested in the modern
idea of Empire; a united Italy was the limit
of his vision; and indeed we often feel, in reading the most important of his works, the *Discourses on the Decades of Livy*, that he has
far more admiration for Republican Rome than
for Imperial Rome. His first thought always
is for peace and prosperity and the happiness
of the governed; but he knows quite well that
this happiness does not reside merely in peace
and wealth. It depends upon, and in turn
supports, the *virtue* of the citizens. Civic virtue cannot exist without a measure of liberty,
and he is constantly concerned with what relative liberty is obtainable:

It seldom happens that the demands of a free people are
either unreasonable or prejudicial to liberty, as they com-
monly proceed either from actual oppression, or the dread
of it; but if that apprehension should prove groundless, it
is no difficult matter to pacify them by a public conference,
where they are always ready to listen to any man of worth
and authority that shall think fit to harangue them: for
though the people may sometimes be in an error, as Tully
says, they are open to better information, and soon con-
vinced, when a person of whose veracity and integrity they
have a good opinion undertakes to show them their mistake.

[54]

Machiavelli's attitude towards religion and towards the religion of his country has often been the object of misunderstanding. His attitude is that of a statesman, and is as noble as that of any statesman, *qua* statesman. In fact, it could be no other than it is. He is opposed neither to religion nor to the Catholic Church. He saw quite clearly, as he could hardly have avoided seeing, the corruption of the Church and the baseness of the eminent ecclesiastics with whom he had to do. And in the *Mandragora*, his brilliant comedy, he makes excellent fun of the more petty corruptions of the priesthood. He saw, on the one hand, the extent to which the Church and the powerful individual nobles of the Church had contributed to the dissension and desolation of his country. But he maintained steadily that an established Church was of the greatest value to a State.

All these things being considered, I conclude, that the introduction of Religion at Rome by Numa was one of the causes that chiefly contributed to its grandeur and felicity: for Religion produced good order, and good order is generally attended with good fortune and success in any undertaking. And, as a strict observance of Divine worship and religious duties always tends to the aggrandizement of a State, so a neglect and contempt of them may be reckoned amongst the first causes of its ruin. For, where there is no fear of God, it must either fall to destruction, or be supported by the reverence shown to a good Prince; which indeed may sustain it for a while, and supply the want of Religion in his Subjects. But as human life is short, the Government must of course sink into decay when the virtue that upheld and informed it is extinct.

And later (in the Discourses) he says still more positively, in words which Archbishop Laud would have approved:

The rulers of all States, whether Kingdoms or Commonwealths, who would preserve their governments firm and entire, ought above all things to take care that Religion is held in the highest veneration, and its ceremonies at all times uncorrupted and inviolable; for there is no surer prognostic of impending ruin in any State, than to see Divine worship neglected or despised.

And he goes on to show, in the same chapter, how the neglect of religion, occasioned by the vagaries of the Church of Rome, had contributed to the ruin of Italy. It is quite possible that an established National Church, such as the Church of England, might have seemed to Machiavelli the best establishment for a Christian commonwealth; but that a religious establishment of some kind is necessary to a

[56]

nation he is quite sure.   If his words were true
then they are true now.   As for Machiavelli's
'personal' religion, it seems to have been as
genuine and sincere as that of any man who is
not a specialist in devotion but intensely a
specialist in statesmanship; and he died with
the ministrations of a priest about him.   He
saw quite clearly and knew instinctively that
the efforts of a man like Savonarola could bring
no good; his real objection was not to the spirit
of Savonarola so much as to the contradiction
between the methods of Savonarola and good
statesmanship.   But with a destructive mind
like that of Voltaire the essentially constructive
mind of Machiavelli could have felt no
community.

In several chapters of *The Prince* and in the
Art of War it is quite clear that in considering
warfare Machiavelli is concerned always with
the positive and the constructive.   In warfare,
and in military government and occupation, he
is interested as much in the moral forces as
in the technical devices.   In his remarks on
colonization, on the manner of occupying a
foreign territory, and in his repeated admoni-
tions against the use of mercenary troops he

is always holding up for admiration the patriot prince and the patriot citizenry. For the prince who is merely a general he has little patience; of an empire like that of Napoleon he would have said at the outset that it could not last. You cannot govern people for ever against their will; and some foreign peoples you cannot rule at all; but if you have to govern an alien and inferior people—a people inferior in the art of government—then you must use every means to make them contented and to persuade them that your government is to their interest. Liberty is good; but more important is order; and the maintenance of order justifies every means. But his soldiers should be citizen soldiers, fighting for something really valuable; and the prince must be a statesman always, and a warrior only when necessary.

No account of Machiavelli's views can be more than fragmentary. For though he is constructive he is not a system builder; and his thoughts can be repeated but not summarized. It is perhaps a character of his amazing exactness of vision and statement that he should have no 'system'; for a system almost inevitably requires slight distortions and omissions, and

[58]

Machiavelli would distort and omit nothing. But what is more curious is that no account or recapitulation of his thought seems to give any clue either to his greatness or to his great and grotesque reputation.   When we first read him we receive the impression neither of a great soul nor of a dæmoniac intellect; but merely of a modest and honest observer setting down matters of fact and comments so true as to be platitudinous.   Only after slow absorption and the repeated contrasts which strike the mind between such honesty and the common deceptions, dishonesties, and tergiversations of the human mind in general does his unique greatness reach us.   We do not imply that Machiavelli's thought is a solitary exception.   A French writer, M. Charles Benoist, has devoted a volume to *Le machiavélisme avant Machiavel*. There are parallels in his own time.   Machiavelli could hardly have known Commynes, but the mind and the vision of the great Belgian diplomat who served Louis of France so long and so well are closely akin to those of Machiavelli.   But Machiavelli, apart from his difference of method, is a far purer and more intense spirit.

The passionate nationalism of Machiavelli was hardly likely to be understood in his own time; least of all by his compatriots. But the honesty of his mind is such as is hardly understood at any time. From the first his writings seem to have fascinated and terrified Europe. From the fascination people could not escape; from the terror they escaped by turning him into a myth of terror. Even in Italy, as Charbonnel shows in *La pensée italienne au XVI siècle*, his thought was immediately distorted. Popes and princes seem to have taken from his books what they wanted, but not what Machiavelli wanted to convey. But as his work penetrated farther abroad the greater became the distortion. In France, and especially among the Huguenots, it aroused the most violent rejoinders. He was treated as hardly more than a clever sycophant giving tips to tyrants on the best ways of oppressing their subjects. In France not only religious partisans but the *politiques*—notably Jean Bodin—fell foul of him. Bodin could not get over Machiavelli's praise of Cæsar Borgia in *The Prince*; although, to anyone who reads the book without prejudice, it should be quite clear in

what respects and with what reservations
Machiavelli bestows his praise. In England
Thomas Cromwell and others admired his
work, though it is quite unlikely that they
understood him better. But the general impression of Machiavelli in England was due
to French influence, to the translation of the
Contre-Machiavel of Gentillet. At every remove Machiavelli suffered. The civilization
of France was in some respects below that of
Italy, and the civilization of England had
certainly not caught up with the civilization of
France. You have only to compare the development of prose style in the three languages.
Machiavelli is a master of prose style of any
age; his prose is *mature*. There is nothing
comparable in France until Montaigne, and
Montaigne is not a *classique* for French
criticism. And there is nothing comparable
in England till Hobbes and Clarendon. But
by that time, when the civilization of the three
countries was much on a level, there is some
deterioration everywhere. Montaigne is inferior to Machiavelli, and Hobbes is inferior to
Montaigne. The dramatization of Machiavelli
in England has been catalogued by Edward

Meyer in his *Machiavelli and the Elizabethan Drama*, and recently discussed more philosophically by Mr. Wyndham Lewis in his extremely interesting study of Shakespeare, *The Lion and the Fox*. The figure of Richard III is the testimony of the impression made by Machiavelli, and the falsity of this impression.

We have therefore to inquire what there is about Machiavelli to impress the mind of Europe so prodigiously and so curiously, and why the European mind felt it necessary to deform his doctrine so absurdly. There are certainly contributing causes. The reputation of Italy as the home of fantastic, wanton and diabolical crime filled the French, and still more the English, imagination as they are now filled by the glories of Chicago or Los Angeles, and predisposed imagination toward the creation of a mythical representative for this criminality. But still more the growth of Protestantism—and France, as well as England, was then largely a Protestant country—created a disposition against a man who accepted in his own fashion the orthodox view of original sin. Calvin, whose view of humanity was far more extreme, and certainly more false, than that of Machiavelli, was never treated to such opprobrium; but when the inevitable reaction against Calvinism came out of Calvinism, and from Geneva, in the doctrine of Rousseau, that too was hostile to Machiavelli. For Machiavelli is a doctor of the mean, and the mean is always insupportable to partisans of the extreme. A fanatic can be tolerated. The failure of a fanaticism such as Savonarola's ensures its toleration by posterity, and even approving patronage. But Machiavelli was no fanatic; he merely told the truth about humanity. The world of human motives which he depicts is true—that is to say, it is humanity without the addition of superhuman Grace. It is therefore tolerable only to persons who have also a definite religious belief; to the effort of the last three centuries to supply religious belief by belief in Humanity the creed of Machiavelli is insupportable. Lord Morley voices the usual modern hostile admiration of Machiavelli when he intimates that Machiavelli saw very clearly what he did see, but that he saw only half of the truth about human nature. What Machiavelli did not see about human nature is the myth of human goodness which for liberal thought replaces the belief in Divine Grace.

It is easy to admire Machiavelli in a sentimental way. It is only one of the sentimental and histrionic poses of human nature—and human nature is incorrigibly histrionic—to pose as a 'realist', a person of 'no nonsense', to admire the 'brutal frankness' or the 'cynicism' of Machiavelli. This is a form of self-satisfaction and self-deception, which merely propagates the Jew of Malta-Nietzsche myth of Machiavelli. In Elizabethan England the reputation of Machiavelli was merely manipulated unconsciously to feed the perpetually recurring tendency to Manichæan heresy: the desire for a devil to worship. The heretical impulses remain fairly constant; they recur in the Satan of Milton and the Cain of Byron. But with these indulgences of human frailties Machiavelli has no traffic. He had none of the instinct to pose; and therefore human beings, in order to accept him at all, had to make him into a dramatic figure. His reputation is the history of the attempt of humanity to protect itself, by secreting a coating of falsehood, against any statement of the truth.

It has been said, in a tone of reproach, that Machiavelli makes no attempt 'to persuade'. Certainly he was no prophet. For he was concerned first of all with truth, not with persuasion, which is one reason why his prose is great prose, not only of Italian but a model of style for any language. He is a partial Aristotle of politics. But he is partial not because his vision is distorted or his judgment biased, or because of any lack of moral interest, but because of his sole passion for the unity, peace, and prosperity of his country. What makes him a great writer, and for ever a solitary figure, is the purity and single-mindedness of his passion. No one was ever less 'Machiavellian' than Machiavelli. Only the pure in heart can blow the gaff on human nature as Machiavelli has done. The cynic can never do it; for the cynic is always impure and sentimental. But it is easy to understand why Machiavelli was not himself a successful politician. For one thing, he had no capacity for self-deception or self-dramatization. The recipe *dors ton sommeil de brute* is applied in many forms, of which Calvin and Rousseau give two variations; but the utility of Machiavelli is his perpetual summons to examination of the weakness and impurity of the soul.   We are not likely to forget his political lessons, but his examination of conscience may be too easily overlooked.

IV

FRANCIS HERBERT BRADLEY

IT is unusual that a book so famous and so influential should remain out of print so long as Bradley's *Ethical Studies*.[1] The one edition appeared in 1876: Bradley's refusal to reprint it never wavered. In 1893, in a footnote in *Appearance and Reality*, and in words characteristic of the man, he wrote: 'I feel that the appearance of other books, as well as the decay of those superstitions against which largely it was directed, has left me free to consult my own pleasure in the matter.' The dates of his three books, the *Ethical Studies* in 1876, the *Principles of Logic* in 1883, and *Appearance and Reality* in 1893, leave us in no doubt that his pleasure was the singular one

[1] *Ethical Studies*. By F. H. Bradley, O.M., LL.D. Second Edition. (Oxford: Clarendon Press. London: Milford.)

[67]

of thinking rather than the common one of
writing books. And Bradley always assumed,
with what will remain for those who did not
know him a curious blend of humility and
irony, an attitude of extreme diffidence about
his own work. His *Ethical Studies*, he told
us (or told our fathers), did not aim at 'the
construction of a system of Moral Philosophy'.
The first words of the preface to his *Principles
of Logic* are: 'The following work makes no
claim to supply any systematic treatment of
logic.' He begins the preface to *Appearance
and Reality* with the words: 'I have described
the following work as an essay in metaphysics.
Neither in form nor extent does it carry out
the idea of a system.' The phrase for each
book is almost the same. And many readers,
having in mind Bradley's polemical irony and
his obvious zest in using it, his habit of dis-
comfiting an opponent with a sudden profes-
sion of ignorance, of inability to understand,
or of incapacity for abstruse thought, have
concluded that this is all a mere pose—and
even a somewhat unscrupulous one. But
deeper study of Bradley's mind convinces us
that the modesty is real, and his irony the

weapon of a modest and highly sensitive man. Indeed, if this had been a pose it would never have worn so well as it has. We have to consider, then, what is the nature of Bradley's influence and why his writings and his personality fascinate those whom they do fascinate; and what are his claims to permanence.

Certainly one of the reasons for the power he still exerts, as well as an indubitable claim to permanence, is his great gift of style. It is for his purposes—and his purposes are more varied than is usually supposed—a perfect style. Its perfection has prevented it from cutting any great figure in prose anthologies and literature manuals, for it is perfectly welded with the matter. Ruskin's works are extremely readable in snippets even for many who take not a particle of interest in the things in which Ruskin was so passionately interested. Hence he survives in anthologies, while his books have fallen into undue neglect. Bradley's books can never fall into this neglect because they will never rise to this notoriety; they come to the hands only of those who are qualified to treat them with respect. But perhaps a profounder difference between a

style like Bradley's and a style like Ruskin's is
a greater purity and concentration of purpose.
One feels that the emotional intensity of Ruskin is partly a deflection of something that was
baffled in life, whereas Bradley, like Newman,
is directly and wholly that which he is. For
the secret of Bradley's style, like that of Berg-
son—whom he resembles in this if in nothing
else—is the intense addiction to an intellectual
passion.

The nearest resemblance in style, however,
is not Ruskin but Matthew Arnold. It has
not been sufficiently observed that Bradley
makes use of the same means as Arnold, and
for similar ends. To take first the most
patent resemblance, we find in Bradley the
same type of fun as that which Arnold has
with his young friend Arminius. In *The
Principles of Logic* there is a celebrated passage
in which Bradley is attacking the theory of
association of ideas according to Professor
Bain, and explains how on this principle an
infant comes to recognize a lump of sugar:

A young child, or one of the lower animals, is given on
Monday a round piece of sugar, eats it and finds it sweet.
On Tuesday it sees a square piece of sugar, and proceeds to

[70]

FRANCIS HERBERT BRADLEY

eat it. . . . Tuesday's sensation and Monday's image are not only separate facts, which, because alike, are therefore *not* the same; but they differ perceptibly both in quality and environment. What is to lead the mind to take one for the other?

Sudden at this crisis, and in pity at distress, there leaves the heaven with rapid wing a goddess Primitive Credulity. Breathing in the ear of the bewildered infant she whispers, The thing which has happened once will happen once more. Sugar was sweet, and sugar will be sweet. And Primitive Credulity is accepted forthwith as the mistress of our life. She leads our steps on the path of experience, until her fallacies, which cannot always be pleasant, at length becomes suspect. We wake up indignant at the kindly fraud by which the goddess so long has deceived us. So she shakes her wings, and flying to the stars, where there are no philosophers, leaves us here to the guidance of—I cannot think what.

This sort of solemn banter is exactly what an admirer of Arnold is ready to enjoy. But it is not only in his fun, or in his middle style, that Bradley is like Arnold; they are alike in their purple passages. The two following may be compared. By Arnold:

And yet, steeped in sentiment as she lies, spreading her gardens to the moonlight, and whispering from her towers the last enchantments of the Middle Age, who will deny that Oxford, by her ineffable charm, keeps ever calling us nearer to the true goal of all of us, to the ideal, to perfection—to beauty, in a word, which is only truth seen from another

[71]

side—nearer, perhaps, than all the science of Tübingen. Adorable dreamer, whose heart has been so romantic! who hast given thyself so prodigally, given thyself to sides and to heroes not mine, only never to the Philistines! home of lost causes, and forsaken beliefs, and unpopular names, and impossible loyalties! what example could ever so inspire us to keep down the Philistine in ourselves, what teacher could ever so save us from that bondage to which we are all prone, that bondage which Goethe, in his incomparable lines on the death of Schiller, makes it his friend's highest praise (and nobly did Schiller deserve the praise) to have left miles out of sight behind him—the bondage of 'was uns alle bändigt, *das Gemeine!*'

The passage from *The Principles of Logic* is not so well known:

It may come from a failure in my metaphysics, or from a weakness of the flesh which continues to blind me, but the notion that existence could be the same as understanding strikes as cold and ghost-like as the dreariest materialism. That the glory of this world in the end is appearance leaves the world more glorious, if we feel it is a show of some fuller splendour; but the sensuous curtain is a deception and a cheat, if it hides some colourless movement of atoms, some spectral woof of impalpable abstractions, or unearthly ballet of bloodless categories. Though dragged to such conclusions, we cannot embrace them. Our principles may be true, but they are not reality. They no more *make* that Whole which commands our devotion than some shredded dissection of human tatters *is* that warm and breathing beauty of flesh which our hearts found delightful.

[72]

Any one who is at all sensitive to style will recognize the similarity of tone and tension and beat. It is not altogether certain that the passage from Bradley is not the better; at any rate such a phrase as Arnold's 'ineffable charm' has not worn at all well.

But if the two men fought with the same weapons—and fundamentally, in spite of Bradley's assault upon Arnold, for the same causes —the weapons of Bradley had behind them a heavier force and a closer precision. Exactly what Bradley fought for and exactly what he fought against have not been quite understood; understanding has been obscured by the dust of Bradley's logical battles. People are inclined to believe that what Bradley did was to demolish the logic of Mill and the psychology of Bain. If he had done that, it would have been a lesser service than what he has done; and if he had done that it would have been less of a service than people think, for there is much that is good in the logic of Mill and the psychology of Bain. But Bradley did not attempt to destroy Mill's logic. Any one who reads his own *Principles* will see that his force is directed not against Mill's logic as a whole but only against certain limitations, imperfections and abuses. He left the structure of Mill's logic standing, and never meant to do anything else. On the other hand, the *Ethical Studies* are not merely a demolition of the Utilitarian theory of conduct but an attack upon the whole Utilitarian mind. For Utilitarianism was, as every reader of Arnold knows, a great temple in Philistia. And of this temple Arnold hacked at the ornaments and cast down the images, and his best phrases remain for ever gibing and scolding in our memory. But Bradley, in his philosophical critique of Utilitarianism, undermined the foundations. The spiritual descendants of Bentham have built anew, as they always will; but at least, in building another temple for the same worship, they have had to apply a different style of architecture. And this is the social basis of Bradley's distinction, and the social basis is even more his claim to our gratitude than the logical basis: he replaced a philosophy which was crude and raw and provincial by one which was, in comparison, catholic, civilized, and universal. True, he was influenced by Kant and Hegel and Lotze. But Kant and Hegel and Lotze are not so despicable as some enthusiastic medievalists would have us believe, and they are, in comparison with the school of Bentham, catholic and civilized and universal. In fighting the battles that he fought in the 'seventies and 'eighties Bradley was fighting for a European and ripened and wise philosophy, against an insular and immature and cranky one; the same battle that Arnold was fighting against the *British Banner*, Judge Edmonds, Newman Weeks, Deborah Butler, Elderess Polly, Brother Noyes, Mr. Murphy, the Licensed Victuallers and the Commercial Travellers.

It is not to say that Arnold's work was vain if we say that it is to be done again; for we must know in advance, if we are prepared for that conflict, that the combat may have truces but never a peace. If we take the widest and wisest view of a Cause, there is no such thing as a Lost Cause because there is no such thing as a Gained Cause. We fight for lost causes because we know that our defeat and dismay may be the preface to our successors' victory, though that victory itself will be temporary; we fight rather to keep something alive than in the expectation that anything will triumph. If Bradley's philosophy is to-day a little out of fashion, we must remark that what has superseded it, what is now in favour, is, for the most part, crude and raw and provincial (though infinitely more technical and scientific) and must perish in its turn. Arnold turned from mid-century Radicalism with the reflection 'A new power has suddenly appeared'. There is always a new power; but the new power destined to supersede the philosophy which has superseded Bradley will probably be something at the same time older, more patient, more supple and more wise. The chief characteristics of much contemporary philosophy are newness and crudeness, impatience, inflexibility in one respect and fluidity in another, and irresponsibility and lack of wisdom. Of wisdom Bradley had a large share; wisdom consists largely of scepticism and uncynical disillusion; and of these Bradley had a large share. And scepticism and disillusion are a useful equipment for religious understanding; and of that Bradley had a share too.

Those who have read the *Ethical Studies* will be ready with the remark that it was

Bradley, in this book and in the year 1876, who knocked the bottom out of *Literature and Dogma*. But that does not mean that the two men were not on the same side; it means only that *Literature and Dogma* is irrelevant to Arnold's main position as given in the Essays and in *Culture and Anarchy*, that the greatest weakness of Arnold's culture was his weakness in philosophical training, and that in philosophical criticism Bradley exhibits the same type of culture that Arnold exhibited in political and social criticism. Arnold had made an excursion into a field for which he was not armed. Bradley's attack upon Arnold does not take up much space, but Bradley was economical of words; it is all in a few paragraphs and a few footnotes to the 'Concluding Remarks':

But here once more 'culture' has come to our aid, and has shown us how here, as everywhere, the study of polite literature, which makes for meekness, makes needless also all further education; and we felt already as if the clouds that metaphysic had wrapped about the matter were dissolving in the light of a fresh and sweet intelligence. And, as we turned towards the dawn, we sighed over poor Hegel, who had read neither Goethe nor Homer, nor the Old and New Testaments, nor any of the literature which has gone to form 'culture', but, knowing no facts, and reading no books, nor ever asking himself 'such a tyro's question as what being really was', sat spinning out of his head those foolish logomachies which impose on no person of refinement.

Here is the identical weapon of Arnold, sharpened to a razor edge and turned against Arnold.

But the 'stream' and the 'tendency' having served their turn, like last week's placards, now fall into the background, and we learn at last that 'the Eternal' is not eternal at all, unless we give that name to whatever a generation sees happen, and believes both has happened and will happen— just as the habit of washing ourselves might be termed 'the Eternal not ourselves that makes for cleanliness', or 'Early to bed and early to rise' the 'Eternal not ourselves that makes for longevity', and so on—that 'the Eternal', in short, is nothing in the world but a piece of literary clap-trap. The consequence is that all we are left with is the assertion that 'righteousness' is 'salvation' or welfare, and that there is a 'law' and a 'Power' which has something to do with this fact; and here again we must not be ashamed to say that we fail to understand what any one of these phrases means, and suspect ourselves once more to be on the scent of clap-trap.

A footnote continues the Arnold-baiting in a livelier style:

'Is there a God?' asks the reader. 'Oh yes,' replies Mr. Arnold, 'and I can verify him in experience.' 'And what is he then?' cries the reader. 'Be virtuous, and as a rule you will be happy,' is the answer. 'Well, and God?' 'That is God,' says Mr. Arnold; 'there is no deception, and what more do you want?' I suppose we do want a good deal more. Most of us, certainly the public which Mr. Arnold addresses, want something they can worship; and they will not find that in an hypostasised copy-book heading, which is not much more adorable than 'Honesty is the best policy', or 'Handsome is that handsome does', or various other edifying maxims, which have not yet come to an apotheosis.

Such criticism is final. It is patently a great triumph of wit and a great delight to watch when a man's methods, almost his tricks of speech, are thus turned against himself. But if we look more closely into these words and into the whole chapter from which they are taken, we find Bradley to have been not only triumphant in polemic but right in reason. Arnold, with all his great virtues, was not always patient enough, or solicitous enough of any but immediate effect, to avoid inconsistency—as has been painstakingly shown by Mr. J. M. Robertson. In *Culture and Anarchy*, which is probably his greatest book, we hear something said about 'the will of God'; but the 'will of God' seems to become superseded in importance by 'our best self, or right reason, to which we want to give authority'; and this best self looks very much like Matthew Arnold slightly disguised. In our own time one of

[79]

the most remarkable of our critics, one who is
fundamentally on most questions in the right,
and very often right quite alone, Professor
Irving Babbitt, has said again and again that
the old curbs of class, of authoritative government, and of religion must be supplied in
our time by something he calls the 'inner
check'. The inner check looks very much
like the 'best self' of Matthew Arnold; and
though supported by wider erudition and
closer reasoning, is perhaps open to the same
objections. There are words of Bradley's, and
in the chapter from which we have already
quoted, that might seem at first sight to support these two eminent doctrines:

> How can the human-divine ideal ever be my will? The
> answer is, Your will it never can be as the will of your private
> self, so that your private self should become wholly good.
> To that self you must die, and by faith be made one with
> that ideal. You must resolve to give up your will, as the
> mere will of this or that man, and you must put your whole
> self, your entire will, into the will of the divine. That must
> be your one self, as it is your true self; that you must hold to
> both with thought and will, and all other you must renounce.

There is one direction in which these words—
and, indeed, Bradley's philosophy as a whole
—might be pushed, which would be danger-

ous; the direction of diminishing the value and dignity of the individual, of sacrificing him to a Church or a State. But, in any event, the words cannot be interpreted in the sense of Arnold. The distinction is not between a 'private self' and a 'public self' or a 'higher self', it is between the individual as himself and no more, a mere numbered atom, and the individual in communion with God. The distinction is clearly drawn between man's 'mere will' and 'the will of the Divine'. It may be noted also that Bradley is careful, in indicating the process, not to exaggerate either will or intellect at the expense of the other. And in all events it is a process which neither Arnold nor Professor Babbitt could accept. But *if* there is a 'will of God', as Arnold, in a hasty moment, admits, then some doctrine of Grace must be admitted too; or else the 'will of God' is just the same inoperative benevolence which we have all now and then received— and resented—from our fellow human beings. In the end it is a disappointment and a cheat.

Those who return to the reading of *Ethical Studies*, and those who now, after reading the other works of Bradley, read it for the first time, will be struck by the unity of Bradley's thought in the three books and in the collected Essays. But this unity is not the unity of mere fixity. In the *Ethical Studies*, for instance, he speaks of the awareness of the self, the knowledge of one's own existence as indubitable and identical. In *Appearance and Reality*, seventeen years later, he had seen much deeper into the matter; and had seen that no one 'fact' of experience in isolation is real or is evidence of anything. The unity of Bradley's thought is not the unity attained by a man who never changes his mind. If he had so little occasion to change it, that is because he usually saw his problems from the beginning in all their complexity and connexions—saw them, in other words, with wisdom—and because he could never be deceived by his own metaphors—which, indeed, he used most sparingly—and was never tempted to make use of current nostrums.

If all of Bradley's writings are in some sense merely 'essays', that is not solely a matter of modesty, or caution, and certainly not of indifference, or even of ill-health. It is that he perceived the contiguity and continuity of the various provinces of thought. 'Reflection on morality,' he says 'leads us beyond it. It leads us, in short, to see the necessity of a religious point of view.' Morality and religion are not the same thing, but they cannot beyond a certain point be treated separately. A system of ethics, if thorough, is explicitly or implicitly a system of theology; and to attempt to erect a complete theory of ethics without a religion is none the less to adopt some particular attitude towards religion. In this book, as in his others, Bradley is thoroughly empirical, much more empirical than the philosophies that he opposed. He wished only to determine how much of morality could be founded securely without entering into the religious questions at all. As in *Appearance and Reality* he assumes that our common everyday knowledge is on the whole true so far as it goes, but that we do not know how far it does go; so in the *Ethical Studies* he starts always with the assumption that our common attitude towards duty, pleasure, or self-sacrifice is correct so far as it goes—but we do not know how far it does go. And in this he is all

in the Greek tradition. It is fundamentally
a philosophy of common sense.

Philosophy without wisdom is vain; and in
the greater philosophers we are usually aware
of that wisdom which for the sake of emphasis
and in the most accurate and profound sense
could be called even worldly wisdom. Common sense does not mean, of course, either the
opinion of the majority or the opinion of the
moment; it is not a thing to be got at without
maturity and study and thought. The lack of
it produces those unbalanced philosophies,
such as Behaviourism, of which we hear a
great deal. A purely 'scientific' philosophy
ends by denying what we know to be true; and,
on the other hand, the great weakness of
Pragmatism is that it ends by being of no *use*
to anybody. Again, it is easy to under-
estimate Hegel, but it is easy to overestimate
Bradley's debt to Hegel; in a philosophy like
Bradley's the points at which he *stops* are always
important points. In an unbalanced or uncul-
tured philosophy words have a way of changing
their meaning—as sometimes with Hegel; or
else they are made, in a most ruthless and
piratical manner, to walk the plank: the words

which Professor J. B. Watson drops over-
board, and which we know to have meaning
and value, are almost innumerable. But Bradley, like Aristotle, is distinguished by his
scrupulous respect for words, that their meaning should be neither vague nor exaggerated;
and the tendency of his labours is to bring
British philosophy closer to the great Greek
tradition.

V

BAUDELAIRE IN OUR TIME

M R. SYMONS has made a good translation, in the Symons style.[1] If our point of view to-day was the point of view of thirty years ago, or even of twenty years ago, we should call it a good translation. To read Mr. Symons now, is to realize how great a man is Baudelaire, who can appear in such a different form to the 'nineties and to the nineteen-twenties. In the translation of Mr. Symons, Baudelaire becomes a poet of the 'nineties, a contemporary of Dowson and Wilde. Dowson and Wilde have passed, and Baudelaire remains; he belonged to a generation that preceded them, and yet he is much more our contemporary than are they. Yet even the 'nineties are nearer to us than the intervening

[1] Baudelaire, *Prose and Poetry*. Translated by Arthur Symons. Albert and Charles Boni.

generation—I date in *literary* generations; and
the fact that they were interested in Baudelaire
indicates some community of spirit. Since
the generation—the *literary* generation—of Mr.
Symons and the 'nineties, another generation
has come and gone—the *literary* generation
which includes Mr. Bernard Shaw, and Mr.
Wells, and Mr. Lytton Strachey. This generation, in its ancestry, 'skipped' the 'nineties:
it is the progeny of Huxley, and Tyndall, and
George Eliot, and Gladstone. And with this
generation Baudelaire has nothing to do; but
he had something to do with the 'nineties, and
he has a great deal to do with us.

But the present volume should perhaps,
even in fairness, be read as a document expli-
catory of the 'nineties, rather than as a current
interpretation of Baudelaire. In an interesting
preface—too short—Mr. Symons avows that
the *Fleurs du Mal* 'in regard to my earliest
verses, was at once a fascination and an influence, and because from that time onward his
fascination has been like a spell to me, and
because that masterpiece has rarely, if ever,
been equalled, has rarely, if ever, been surpassed'. Mr. Symons is himself, we must

remember, no mean poet; he is typical of the 'nineties; this influence of Baudelaire upon Mr. Symons was manifestly genuine and profound. Why is Baudelaire so different now? We can learn something about Baudelaire, and about the 'nineties, and about ourselves.

Mr. Symons's preface is very interesting: it is perhaps the most important part of the book. What is interesting is the attitude, so completely of his epoch, toward 'vice'. For Mr. Symons there is, at least *en principe*, a ritual, an hierarchy, a liturgy, of 'vice' or 'sin'. Here is a whole paragraph so significant that I beg to give it entire:

In the poetry of Baudelaire, with which the poetry of Verlaine is so often compared [*i.e. compared by Mr. Symons and his friends—we no longer find much in common*] there is a deliberate science of sensual and sexual perversity which has something curious in its accentuation of vice with horror, in its passionate devotion to passions. Baudelaire brings every complication of taste, the exasperation of perfumes, the irritant of cruelty, the very odours and colours of corruption, to the creation and adornment of a sort of religion, in which an Eternal Mass is served before a veiled altar. There is no confession, no absolution, not a prayer is permitted which is not set down on the ritual. . . . 'To cultivate one's hysteria' I have written 'so calmly, and to affront the reader (*Hypocrite lecteur, mon semblable, mon frère*) as a judge rather

BAUDELAIRE IN OUR TIME

than a penitent; to be a casuist in confession; to be so much a moralist, with so keen and so subtle a sense of the ecstasy of evil: that has always bewildered the world, even in his own country, where the artist is allowed to live as experimentally as he writes. Baudelaire lived and died solitary, secret, a confessor of sins who had never told the whole truth, *le mauvais moine* of his own sonnet, an ascetic of passion, a hermit of the Brothel.'

This paragraph is of extraordinary interest for several reasons. Even in its cadences it conjures up Wilde and the remoter spectre of Pater. It conjures up also Lionel Johnson with his 'life is a ritual'. It cannot get away from religion and religious figures of speech. How different a tone from that of the generation of Mr. Shaw,[1] and Mr. Wells, and Mr. Strachey, and Mr. Ernest Hemingway! And how different from our own! Mr. Symons seems to us like a sensitive child, who has been taken into a church, and has been entranced with the effigies, and the candles, and the incense. *Such rugs and jugs and candle lights!*
And indeed the age of Mr. Symons was the

[1] Of course Mr. Shaw and Mr. Wells are also much occupied with religion and *Ersatz-Religion*. But they are concerned with the spirit, not the letter. And the spirit killeth, but the letter giveth life.

'golden age' of one kind of child, as the age of Mr. Shaw was the age of another kind of child. If you take his paragraph to pieces, you will find much that is wrong; though if you swallow it whole, you will digest something that is right. '*Passionate devotion to passions*': no man was ever less the dupe of passions than Baudelaire; he was engaged in an attempt to explain, to justify, to make something of them, an enterprise which puts him almost on a level with the author of the 'Vita Nuova.' '*The irritant of cruelty*'—did Baudelaire 'bring' it, or did he not merely examine it (there are some important paragraphs in *Mon Coeur Mis à Nu*). Whoever heard of a Mass before a veiled altar? And hysteria! was any one ever less hysterical, more lucid, than Baudelaire? [1] There is a difference between hysteria and looking into the Shadow. And when Mr. Symons says, a few pages later, that Baudelaire's 'impeccable' work is 'the direct result of his heredity and of his nerves' I can only protest violently.

[1] It is true that Baudelaire says '*J'ai cultivé mon hystérie.*' But it is one thing for him to say it of himself, another for Mr. Symons to say it about him.

If any work is to be described as the 'direct' result of heredity and nerves—and 'direct' here can only suggest that heredity and nerves sufficiently account for the work—then I cannot agree that such work is impeccable. We cannot be *primarily* interested in any writer's nerves (and remember please that 'nerves' used in this way is a very vague and unscientific term) or in any one's heredity except for the purpose of knowing to what extent that writer's individuality distorts or detracts from the objective truth which he perceives. If a writer sees truly—as far as he sees at all—then his heredity and nerves do not matter.[1] What is right in Mr. Symons's account is the impression it gives that Baudelaire was primarily occupied with religious values. What is wrong is the childish attitude of the 'nineties toward religion, the belief—which is no more than the game of children dressing up and playing at being grown-ups—that there is a religion of Evil, or Vice, or Sin. Swinburne knew nothing about Evil, or Vice, or Sin—if he had known anything he would not have had so

[1] There is a better, and very interesting, account of Baudelaire's heredity in Léon Daudet's book, *L'Hérédo*.

much fun out of it. For Swinburne's disciples, the men of the 'nineties, Evil was very
good fun. Experience, as a sequence of
outward events, is nothing in itself; it is
possible to pass through the most terrible
experiences protected by histrionic vanity;
Wilde, through the whole of the experiences of
his life, remained a little Eyas, a child-actor.
On the other hand, even to act an important
thing is to acknowledge it; and the childishness
of the 'nineties is nearer to reality than the
childishness of the nineteen-hundreds. But to
Baudelaire, alone, these things were real.

Mr. Symons appears a more childish child
than Huysmans, merely because a childish
Englishman—bred a Protestant—always appears more childish than a childish French-
man—bred a Roman. Huysmans's fee-fi-fo-
fum *décor* of mediævalism has nothing on Mr.
Symons's 'veiled altar'. Huysmans, by the
way, might have been much more in sympathy
with the real spirit of the thirteenth century
if he had thought less about it, and bothered
less about architectural lore and quotations
from philosophers whom he may have read but
certainly did not understand: he is much more

'mediæval' (and much more human) when he describes the visit of Madame Chantelouve to Durtal than when he talks about his Cathedral.

I have already suggested that Mr. Symons, as a translator, turns Baudelaire into a contemporary of Symons. To say this is at once a very high compliment—for the work of translation is to make something foreign, or something remote in time, live with our own life, and no translator can endow his victim with more abundant life than he possesses himself—and a warning. It is not a warning against Mr. Symons as translator. Mr. Symons is as true a translator as Mr. Symons can be. That is to say that his translation is, from his own point of view, almost perfect; we have no suggestions to make to Mr. Symons himself. Only, it is what Baudelaire means to Mr. Symons's generation; it is not what Baudelaire means to us. For one thing, we now are much better qualified to appreciate the very traditional character of Baudelaire's verse; we are nearer to Racine than is Mr. Symons; and if we translated Baudelaire ourselves we should bring out just those resemblances to Racine which disappear com-

pletely in Mr. Symons's translation. It is a
pity that Mr. Symons has not translated some
of the poems in which this affinity with Racine
is most apparent. The poet who wrote

> *Andromaque, des bras d'un grand époux tombée,*
> *Vil bétail, sous la main du superbe Pyrrhus* . . .
>
> *De l'ancien Frascati vestale enamourée* . . .
>
> *Nos Pylades là-bas tendent leurs bras vers nous.*
> *'Pour rafraîchir ton coeur nage vers ton Electre!'* . . .

is not remote from the poet who wrote of
'*La fille de Minos et Pasiphaë* . . .' We can,
however, call attention to passages where it
seems to us that Mr. Symons has enveloped
Baudelaire in the Swinburnian violet-coloured
London fog of the 'nineties. His paraphrase
of 'L'Invitation au Voyage' is significant.

> My child and my star,
> Let us wander afar . . .

Baudelaire wrote

> *Mon enfant, ma soeur,*
> *Songe à la douceur*
> *D'aller là-bas vivre ensemble.*

The word *soeur* here is not, in my opinion,
chosen merely because it rhymes with *douceur;*

it is a moment in that sublimation of passion toward which Baudelaire was always striving; it needs a commentary out of his Correspondence, for instance the astonishing letter to Marie X . . . cited by Charles Du Bos.[1]   (On this whole subject Du Bos, whose essay on Baudelaire is the finest study of Baudelaire that has been made, has some admirable words: *ce désir contemplatif qui n'a besoin que de la présence, et qui ne possède vraiment que parce qu'il ne possède pas.*)   And further on, in the same poem, when we come to the magnificent lines

> *Là, tout n'est qu'ordre et beauté,*
> *Luxe, calme et volupté*

we are surprised to receive from Mr. Symons

> There all is beauty, ardency,
> Passion, rest and luxury.

The only one of these words that is right is 'beauty'.   Baudelaire did not, we may be sure, take these substantives at random, nor did he arrange them at random.   It is not for nothing that he put *ordre* first; and if Mr. Symons had

[1] Charles Du Bos, *Approximations*, p. 219.

understood *notre* Baudelaire he would not have substituted—'ardency'! But order is positive, chaos is defect, and we imagine that Mr. Symons was not trying to *avoid* Order—he simply did not recognize it. We can see that Mr. Symons, trained in the verbal school of Swinburne, is simply anxious to get a nice sounding phrase; and we infer that all that he found in Baudelaire was a nice sounding phrase. But Baudelaire was not a disciple of Swinburne: for Baudelaire every word counts.

Here is another passage where Mr. Symons seems to me merely to have made a smudgy botch. It is striking because it is Baudelaire in his most sardonic, bathetic vein—something which might be called strictly 'modern', and which should therefore (considering that Mr. Symons belongs to a younger generation than Baudelaire) have appealed to Mr. Symons. These are well-known lines from the 'Voyage à Cythère'.

> *Quelle est cette île triste et noire? C'est Cythère,*
> *Nous dit-on, un pays fameux dans les chansons,*
> *Eldorado banal de tous les vieux garçons.*
> *Regardez, après tout, c'est une pauvre terre.*

Mr. Symons astounds us with the following:

> What is this sad dark Isle? It is Cythera whose birth
> Was famed in songs, made famous as the fashions
> Of the most ancient and adulterous passions:
> It is a beautiful and a barren earth.

Here Mr. Symons's 'stretchèd metre', always reminiscent of Cynara, fits Baudelaire's deliberately broken alexandrines better than it does in many places (in many of the poems, one feels that Pope would have been better fitted than Mr. Symons). But such a mistranslation cannot be merely a confession of impotence to translate the words of Baudelaire into English; it expresses an impotence to *feel* the moods of Baudelaire—they can be expressed in English just as well as in French—an impotence to use words definitely, to use words at all unless they are the few poor counters of habitual and lazy sentiment. *Fashions and Passions*—how well we know them!

The important fact about Baudelaire is that he was essentially a Christian, born out of his due time, and a classicist, born out of his due time. In his verse technique, he is nearer to Racine than to Mr. Symons; in his sensibility, he is near to Dante and not without

[97]　　G

sympathy with Tertullian. But Baudelaire
was not an aesthetic or a political Christian;
his tendency to 'ritual', which Mr. Symons,
with his highly acute but blind sensibility, has
observed, springs from no attachment to the
outward forms of Christianity, but from the
instincts of a soul that was *naturaliter* Christian. And being the kind of Christian that
he was, born when he was, he had to discover
Christianity for himself. In this pursuit he
was alone in the solitude which is only known
to saints. To him the notion of Original
Sin came spontaneously, and the need for
prayer.

> *Tout chez Baudelaire est fonction de son génie; or il n'y a
> rien dont ce génie puisse moins se passer que de Dieu,—d'un
> Dieu qui plutôt qu'objet de foi est réceptacle de prières,—j'irai
> jusqu'à dire d'un Dieu qu'on puisse prier sans croire en lui. . . .
> Cet incoercible besoin de prière au sein même de l'incrédulité,—
> signe majeur d'une âme marquée de christianisme, qui jamais ne
> lui échappera tout à fait. La notion de péché, et plus profonde-
> ment encore le besoin de prière, telles sont les deux réalités
> souterraines qui paraissent appartenir à des gisements enfouis
> bien plus avant que ne l'est la foi elle-même. On se rappelle le
> mot de Flaubert: 'Je suis mystique au fond et je ne crois à
> rien'; Baudelaire et lui se sont toujours fraternellement compris.*

So far Charles Du Bos. Other essays, not so
satisfactory as that of M. Du Bos, but recent

and explanatory of Baudelaire as he is now understood, are 'Notre Baudelaire' by Stanislas Fumet, and 'La Vie Douloureuse de Baudelaire' by François Porché.

And Baudelaire came to attain the greatest, the most difficult, of the Christian virtues, the virtue of humility. Only by devoted study of the man and his work and his life can we appreciate the significance of that great passage in *Mon Coeur Mis à Nu*:

Faire tous les matins ma prière à Dieu, réservoir de toute force et de toute justice, à mon père, à Mariette et à Poë, comme intercesseurs; les prier de me communiquer la force nécessaire pour accomplir tous mes devoirs, et d'octroyer à ma mère une vie assez longue pour jouir de ma transformation; travailler toute la journée, ou du moins tant que mes forces me le permettront; me fier à Dieu, c'est-à-dire à la Justice même, pour la réussite de mes projets; faire, tous les soirs, une nouvelle prière, pour demander à Dieu la vie et la force pour ma mère et pour moi; faire, de tout ce que je gagnerai, quatre parts,—une pour la vie courante, une pour mes créanciers, une pour mes amis et une pour ma mère;—obéir aux principes de la plus stricte sobriété, dont le premier est la suppression de tous les excitants, quels qu'ils soient.

VI

THOMAS MIDDLETON

THOMAS MIDDLETON, the dramatic writer,
was not very highly thought of in his own
time; the date of his death is not known; we
know only that he was buried on July 4, 1627.
He was one of the more voluminous, and one
of the best, dramatic writers of his time. But
it is easy to understand why he is not better
known or more popular. It is difficult to
imagine his 'personality'. Several new personalities have recently been fitted to the name
of Shakespeare; Jonson is a real figure—our
imagination plays about him discoursing at
the Mermaid, or laying down the law to
Drummond of Hawthornden; Chapman has
become a breezy British character as firm as
Nelson or Wellington; Webster and Donne are
real people for the more intellectual; even
Tourneur (Churton Collins having said the

last word about him) is a 'personality'. But Middleton, who collaborated shamelessly, who is hardly separated from Rowley, Middleton, who wrote plays so diverse as *Women Beware Women* and *A Game at Chesse* and *The Roaring Girl*, Middleton remains merely a collective name for a number of plays—some of which, like *The Spanish Gypsy*, are patently by other people.[1]

If we write about Middleton's plays we must write about Middleton's plays, and not about Middleton's personality. Many of these plays are still in doubt. Of all the Elizabethan dramatists Middleton seems the most impersonal, the most indifferent to personal fame or perpetuity, the readiest, except Rowley, to accept collaboration. Also he is the most various. His greatest tragedies and his greatest comedies are as if written by two different men. Yet there seems no doubt that Middleton was both a great comic writer and a great tragic writer. There are a sufficient number of plays, both tragedies and comedies, in which his hand is so far unquestioned, to establish

[1] Mr. Dugdale Sykes has written authoritatively on this subject.

his greatness. His greatness is not that of a peculiar personality, but of a great artist or artisan of the Elizabethan epoch. We have among others *The Changeling*, *Women Beware Women*, and *A Game at Chesse*; and we have *The Roaring Girl* and *A Trick to Catch the Old One*. And that is enough. Between the tragedies and the comedies of Shakespeare, and certainly between the tragedies and the comedies of Jonson, we can establish a relation; we can see, for Shakespeare or Jonson, that each had in the end a personal point of view which can be called neither comic nor tragic. But with Middleton we can establish no such relation. He remains merely a name, a voice, the author of certain plays, which are all of them great plays. He has no point of view, is neither sentimental nor cynical; he is neither resigned, nor disillusioned, nor romantic; he has no message. He is merely the name which associates six or seven great plays.

For there is no doubt about *The Changeling*. Like all of the plays attributed to Middleton, it is long-winded and tiresome; the characters talk too much, and then suddenly stop talking and act; they are real and impelled

irresistibly by the fundamental motions of
humanity to good or evil. This mixture of
tedious discourse and sudden reality is everywhere in the work of Middleton, in his comedy
also. In *The Roaring Girl* we read with toil
through a mass of cheap conventional intrigue,
and suddenly realize that we are, and have
been for some time without knowing it,
observing a real and unique human being.
In reading *The Changeling* we may think, till
almost the end of the play, that we have been
concerned merely with a fantastic Elizabethan
morality, and then discover that we are looking
on at an impassionate exposure of fundamental
passions of any time and any place. The
usual opinion remains the just judgment:
The Changeling is Middleton's greatest play.
The morality of the convention seems to us
absurd. To many intelligent readers this
play has only an historical interest, and only
serves to illustrate the moral taboos of the
Elizabethans. The heroine is a young woman
who, in order to dispose of a fiancê to whom
she is indifferent, so that she may marry the
man she loves, accepts the offer of an adven-
turer to murder the affianced, at the price of

becoming the murderer's mistress. Such a
plot is, to a modern mind, absurd; and the
consequent tragedy seems a fuss about nothing.
But *The Changeling* is not merely contingent
for its effect upon our acceptance of Elizabethan good form or convention; it is, in fact,
no more dependent upon the convention of its
epoch than a play like *A Doll's House*. Underneath the convention there is the stratum
of permanent truth to human nature. The
tragedy of *The Changeling* is an eternal tragedy,
as permanent as *Œdipus* or *Antony and Cleo-
patra*; it is the tragedy of the not naturally
bad but irresponsible and undeveloped nature,
caught in the consequences of its own action.
In every age and in every civilization there
are instances of the same thing: the unmoral
nature, suddenly trapped in the inexorable
toils of morality—of morality not made by
man but by Nature—and forced to take
the consequences of an act which it had
planned light-heartedly. Beatrice is not a
moral creature; she becomes moral only by
becoming damned. Our conventions are not
the same as those which Middleton assumed
for his play. But the possibility of that

frightful discovery of morality remains permanent.

The words in which Middleton expresses
his tragedy are as great as the tragedy. The
process through which Beatrice, having decided
that De Flores is the instrument for her purpose, passes from aversion to habituation,
remains a permanent commentary on human
nature. The directness and precision of De
Flores are masterly, as is also the virtuousness
of Beatrice on first realizing his motives—

> Why, 'tis impossible thou canst be so wicked,
> Or shelter such a cunning cruelty,
> To make his death the murderer of my honour!
> Thy language is so bold and vicious,
> I cannot see which way I can forgive it
> With any modesty

—a passage which ends with the really great
lines of De Flores, lines of which Shakespeare
or Sophocles might have been proud:

> Can you weep Fate from its determined purpose?
> So soon may you weep me.

But what constitutes the essence of the tragedy
is something which has not been sufficiently
remarked; it is the *habituation* of Beatrice

to her sin; it becomes no longer sin but merely custom.   Such is the essence of the tragedy of *Macbeth*—the habituation to crime, the deadening of all moral sense.   And in the end Beatrice, having been so long the enforced conspirator of De Flores, becomes (and this is permanently true to human nature) more *his* partner, *his* mate, than the mate and partner of the man for the love of whom she consented to the crime.   Her lover disappears not only from the scene but from her own imagination. When she says of De Flores,

> A wondrous necessary man, my lord,

her praise is more than half sincere; and at the end she belongs far more to De Flores— towards whom, at the beginning, she felt strong physical repulsion—than to her lover Alsemero.   It is De Flores, in the end, to whom she belongs as Francesca to Paolo:

> Beneath the stars, upon yon meteor
> Ever hung my fate, 'mongst things corruptible;
> I ne'er could pluck it from him; my loathing
> Was prophet to the rest, but ne'er believed.

And De Flores's cry is perfectly sincere and in character:

I loved this woman in spite of her heart;
Her love I earned out of Piracquo's murder . . .
Yes, and her honour's prize
Was my reward; I thank life for nothing
But that pleasure; it was so sweet to me,
That I have drunk up all, left none behind
For any man to pledge me.

The tragedy of Beatrice is not that she has lost Alsemero, for whose possession she played; it is that she has won De Flores. Such tragedies are not limited to Elizabethan times: they happen every day and perpetually. The greatest tragedies are occupied with great and permanent moral conflicts: the great tragedies of Æschylus, of Sophocles, of Corneille, of Racine, of Shakespeare have the same burden. In poetry, in dramatic technique, *The Changeling* is inferior to the best plays of Webster. But in the moral essence of tragedy it is safe to say that in this play Middleton is surpassed by one Elizabethan alone, and that is Shakespeare. In some respects in which Elizabethan tragedy can be compared to French or to Greek tragedy *The Changeling* stands above every tragic play of its time, except those of Shakespeare.

The genius which blazed in *The Changeling*

[107]

was fitful but not accidental.   The best tragedy
after *The Changeling* is *Women Beware Women*.
The thesis of the play, as the title indicates,
is more arbitrary and less fundamental.   The
play itself, although less disfigured by ribaldry
or clowning, is more tedious.   Middleton
sinks himself in conventional moralizing of the
epoch; so that, if we are impatient, we decide
that he gives merely a document of Elizabethan
humbug—and then suddenly a personage will
blaze out in genuine fire of vituperation.   The
wickedness of the personages in *Women Beware
Women* is conventional wickedness of the stage
of the time; yet slowly the exasperation of
Bianca, the wife who married beneath her,
beneath the ambitions to which she was entitled,
emerges from the negative; slowly the real
human passions emerge from the mesh of
interest in which they begin.   And here again
Middleton, in writing what appears on the
surface a conventional picture-palace Italian
melodrama of the time, has caught permanent
human feelings.   And in this play Middleton
shows his interest—more than any of his con-
temporaries—in innuendo and double meanings; and makes use of that game of chess,

which he was to use more openly and directly for satire in that perfect piece of literary political art, *A Game at Chesse*. The irony could not be improved upon:

> Did I not say my duke would fetch you o'er, Widow?
> I think you spoke in earnest when you said it, madam.
> And my black king makes all the haste he can too.
> Well, madam, we may meet with him in time yet.
> I've given thee blind mate twice.

There is hardly anything truer or more impressive in Elizabethan drama than Bianca's gradual self-will and self-importance in consequence of her courtship by the Duke:

> Troth, you speak wondrous well for your old house here;
> 'Twill shortly fall down at your feet to thank you,
> Or stoop, when you go to bed, like a good child,
> To ask you blessing.

In spite of all the long-winded speeches, in spite of all the conventional Italianate horrors, Bianca remains, like Beatrice in *The Changeling*, a real woman; as real, indeed, as any woman of Elizabethan tragedy. Bianca is a type of the woman who is purely moved by vanity.

But if Middleton, this obscure and unin-

teresting person, understood the female better
than any of the Elizabethans—better than the
creator of the Duchess of Malfy, better than
Marlowe, better than Tourneur, or Shirley,
or Fletcher, better than any of them except
Shakespeare alone—he was also able, in his
comedy, to present a finer woman than any
of them. *The Roaring Girl* has no apparent
relation to Middleton's tragedies, yet it is
agreed to be primarily the work of Middleton.
It is typical of the comedies of Middleton, and
it is the best. In his tragedies Middleton
employs all the Italianate horrors of his time,
and obviously for the purpose of pleasing the
taste of his time; yet underneath we feel always
a quiet and undisturbed vision of things as
they are and not 'another thing'. So in his
comedies. The comedies are long-winded; the
fathers are heavy fathers, and rant as heavy
fathers should; the sons are wild and wanton
sons, and perform all the pranks to be expected of them; the machinery is the usual
Elizabethan machinery; Middleton is solicitous to please his audience with what they
expect; but there is underneath the same
steady impersonal passionless observation of

human nature. *The Roaring Girl* is as artificial as any comedy of the time; its plot creaks loudly; yet the Girl herself is always real. She may rant, she may behave preposterously, but she remains a type of the sort of woman who has renounced all happiness for herself and who lives only for a principle. Nowhere more than in *The Roaring Girl* can the hand of Middleton be distinguished more clearly from the hand of Dekker. Dekker is all sentiment; and, indeed, in the so admired passages of *A Fair Quarrel*, exploited by Lamb, the mood if not the hand of Dekker seems to the unexpert critic to be more present than Middleton's. *A Fair Quarrel* seems as much, if not more, Dekker's than Middleton's. Similarly with *The Spanish Gypsy*, which can with difficulty be attributed to Middleton. But the feeling about Moll Cut-Purse of *The Roaring Girl* is Middleton's rather than anybody's. In Middleton's tragedy there is a strain of realism underneath, which is one with the poetry; and in his comedy we find the same thing.

In her recent book on *The Social Mode of Restoration Comedy*, Miss Kathleen Lynch calls

attention to the gradual transition from Elizabethan-Jacobean to Restoration comedy. She
observes, what is certainly true, that Middleton
is the greatest 'realist' in Jacobean comedy.
Miss Lynch's extremely suggestive thesis is
that the transition from Elizabethan-Jacobean
to later Caroline comedy is primarily economic:
that the interest changes from the citizen
aping gentry to the citizen become gentry
and accepting that code of manners. In the
comedy of Middleton certainly there is as yet
no code of manners; but the merchant of
Cheapside is *aiming* at becoming a member of
the county gentry. Miss Lynch remarks:
'Middleton's keen concentration on the spectacle of the interplay of different social classes
marks an important development in realistic
comedy.' She calls attention to this aspect of
Middleton's comedy, that it marks, better
than the romantic comedy of Shakespeare, or
the comedy of Jonson, occupied with what
Jonson thought to be permanent and not tran-
sient aspects of human nature, the transition
between the aristocratic world which preceded
the Tudors and the plutocratic modern world
which the Tudors initiated and encouraged.

By the time of the return of Charles II, as Miss Lynch points out, society had been reorganized and formed, and social conventions had been created. In the Tudor times birth still counted (though nearly all the great families were extinct); by the time of Charles II only breeding counted. The comedy of Middleton, and the comedy of Brome, and the comedy of Shirley, is intermediate, as Miss Lynch remarks. Middleton, she observes, marks the transitional stage in which the London tradesman was anxious to cease to be a tradesman and to become a country gentleman. The words of his City Magnate in *Michaelmas Terme* have not yet lost their point:

A fine journey in the Whitsun holydays, i'faith, to ride with a number of cittizens and their wives, some upon pillions, some upon side-saddles, I and little Thomasine i' the middle, our son and heir, Sim Quomodo, in a peach-colour taffeta jacket, some horse length, or a long yard before us—there will be a fine show on's I can tell you.

But Middleton's comedy is not, like the comedy of Congreve, the comedy of a set social behaviour; it is still, like the later comedy of

[113]   H

Dickens, the comedy of individuals, in spite of the continual motions of city merchants towards county gentility. In the comedy of the Restoration a figure such as that of Moll Cut-Purse would have been impossible. As a social document the comedy of Middleton illustrates the transition from government by a landed aristocracy to government by a city aristocracy gradually engrossing the land. As such it is of the greatest interest. But as literature, as a dispassionate picture of human nature, Middleton's comedy deserves to be remembered chiefly by its real—perpetually real—and human figure of Moll the Roaring Girl. That Middleton's comedy was 'photographic', that it introduces us to the low life of the time far better than anything in the comedy of Shakespeare or the comedy of Jonson, better than anything except the pamphlets of Dekker and Greene and Nashe, there is little doubt. But it produced one great play—*The Roaring Girl*—a great play in spite of the tedious long speeches of some of the principal characters, in spite of the clumsy machinery of the plot: for the reason that Middleton was a great observer of human nature, without fear, without sentiment, without prejudice, without personality.

And Middleton in the end—after criticism has subtracted all that Rowley, all that Dekker, all that others contributed—is a great example of great English drama. He has no message; he is merely a great recorder. Incidentally, in flashes and when the dramatic need comes, he is a great poet, a great master of versification:

> I that am of your blood was taken from you
> For your better health; look no more upon 't,
> But cast it to the ground regardlessly,
> Let the common sewer take it from distinction:
> Beneath the stars, upon yon meteor
> Ever hung my fate, 'mongst things corruptible;
> I ne'er could pluck it from him; my loathing
> Was prophet to the rest, but ne'er believed.

The man who wrote these lines remains inscrutable, solitary, unadmired; purely an Elizabethan and not himself; welcoming collaboration, indifferent to fame; dying no one knows when and no one knows how; attracting, in three hundred years, no personal admiration. Yet he wrote one tragedy which more than

any play except those of Shakespeare has a
profound and permanent moral value and
horror; and one comedy which more than
any Elizabethan comedy realizes a free and
noble womanhood.

VII

A NOTE ON RICHARD CRASHAW

No higher compliment can be paid to this book [1] than to say that in editing and in production it is worthy of the fine series of seventeenth-century poets of which it is a member. Memorable in this series are Saintsbury's 'Caroline Poets' (without which Benlowes, Cleveland, and King would be almost inaccessible), Grierson's 'Donne', Margoliouth's 'Marvell', and Professor Martin's own 'Vaughan'. This edition of Crashaw was much needed. Heretofore the only scholarly edition was that of Waller, in 1904. It was a good edition for its time; but the text was neither well established nor complete; and for an ordinary reader it had the disadvantage that one sometimes had to hunt to find the poem

[1] *The Poems English Latin and Greek of Richard Crashaw.* Edited by L. C. Martin. Oxford University Press.

one wanted. Mr. Martin has collated the texts and gives the variants, without disfiguring the pages of a very handsome and practical book. His notes deserve particular attention, for Crashaw is a poet who needs notes—not for reading for pleasure—but if we wish to study him in relation to his time. Poets of that age made use of each other pretty freely; Crashaw for one was well read (thanks partly to his father's library) in the Italian and Latin poetry of his time, which was Legion. Mr. Martin's notes give many interesting parallels. If there is anything more to be discovered about Crashaw, it will be in the way of further derivations.

Having given due praise to the edition, I must confess to some disappointment with the introduction. It gives a very dense summary of the facts, and includes an extremely interesting letter written by Crashaw. But Mr. Martin seems over-anxious not to use too much space: on the other hand the one critical opinion on which he ventures does not seem to me happy. Perhaps I expected, in default of any critical biography of Crashaw, something that would take its place; something as good as Grierson's capital study of Donne in his edition of that poet above mentioned. We are still left with no first-rate criticism of Crashaw in English. The best study of Crashaw that I know, and a very fine and suggestive essay, is that by Mario Praz in his *Secentismo e Marinismo in Inghilterra.*

'When we survey' says Professor Martin, 'the remarkable development of Crashaw's genius close up to the end of his life, in circumstances that must often have been trying and distracting in the extreme, his "unfulfilled renown" becomes indeed comparable with that of those other two English poets whose work his own in some ways strangely foreshadows, and who, like him, found in Italy a retreat and a final resting place.' (I wish Mr. Martin had saved a line or two by saying Keats and Shelley straight out, instead of searching for a fine phrase.) Now this remark might lead to several false inferences. Crashaw lived to be about thirty-seven; so he had some good years more than Keats or Shelley in which to develop. A man can go far between twenty-seven and thirty-seven. Mr. Martin is therefore unfair to Keats and Shelley. But moreover Crashaw's verse is, as one would expect, far more mature than that of either of these poets; and I do not find in the poem on which he bases this suggestion, the 'Letter to the Countess of Denbigh', the evidence of *promise* that Mr. Martin finds in it. It is indeed a fine poem, but it is the work of a mature master, and promises nothing but more of the same kind. Crashaw is, I believe, a much greater poet than he is usually supposed to be; Keats and Shelley are, in their actual accomplishment, not nearly such great poets as they are supposed to be. But nothing that Crashaw wrote has the *promise* that is patent in *Hyperion* or *The Triumph of Life*. We must try of course always to distinguish promise from performance; both must be taken into account in judging a poet, and they must be kept separate. We can only say that Keats and Shelley would *probably* have become greater poets, poets on a much greater scale, than Crashaw; judging them on their accomplishment only, Crashaw was a finished master, and Keats and Shelley were apprentices with immense possibilities before them.

So much for one question. Next, in what

way can Crashaw be said to 'foreshadow' Keats
and Shelley? As for Keats, I simply do not
know what Mr. Martin means, I see so little
resemblance.   With Shelley, there are obvious
and striking resemblances, though I think very
superficial ones.   To suggest, as Mr. Martin's
words seem to me to suggest, that Crashaw
was in any way a forerunner or 'prophet' of
Shelley, is quite off the rails.   The obvious
parallel is between 'The Weeper' and 'The
Skylark', rather than between their uses of
the octosyllabic couplet, which are wholly
different.

> The dew no more will weepe,
> The Primroses pale cheeke to decke,
> The deaw no more will sleepe,
> Nuzzel'd in the Lillies neck.
> Much rather would it tremble heere,
> And leave them both to bee thy Teare.

> Not the soft Gold which
> Steales from the Amber-weeping Tree,
> Makes sorrow halfe so Rich,
> As the drops distil'd from thee.
> Sorrowes best Iewels lye in these
> Caskets, of which Heaven keeps the Keyes.

. . . .

[121]

> Not in the Evenings Eyes
> When they red with weeping are,
> For the Sun that dyes,
> Sits sorrow with a face so faire.
> Nowhere but heere did ever meet
> Sweetnesse so sad, sadnes so sweet.

I doubt whether the *sound* of two poems can be very similar, when the *sense* is entirely different. At any rate, I have found that the more I studied the meaning of Crashaw's verse, and his peculiar use of image and conceit, the less resemblance the music of it seemed to have to Shelley's. Take one of Crashaw's more extreme and grotesque figures, from 'The Tear':

> Faire Drop, why quak'st thou so?
> 'Cause thou streight must lay thy Head
> In the Dust? o no;
> The Dust shall never bee thy Bed:
> A pillow for thee will I bring,
> Stuft with Downe of Angels wing.

This imagery is almost the quintessence of an immense mass of devotional verse of the seventeenth century. But it has nothing to do with Shelley. Crashaw's images, even when entirely preposterous—for there is no warrant for bringing a pillow (and what a pillow!) for

[122]

the *head* of a *tear*—give a kind of intellectual pleasure—it is a deliberate conscious perversity of language, a perversity like that of the amazing and amazingly impressive interior of St. Peter's. There is brain work in it. But in 'The Skylark' there is no brain work. For the first time perhaps in verse of such eminence, sound exists without sense. Crashaw would never have written so shabby a line as 'That from heaven or near it' merely to provide an imperfect rhyme for *spirit*.

> Keen as are the arrows
> Of that silver sphere
> Whose intense lamp narrows
> In the white dawn clear,
> Until we hardly see, we feel that it is there.

I should be grateful for any explanation of this stanza; until now I am still ignorant to what Sphere Shelley refers, or why it should have silver arrows, or what the devil he means by an intense lamp narrowing in the white dawn; though I can understand that we could hardly see the lamp of a *silver* sphere narrowing in *white* dawn (why dawn? as he has just referred to the pale purple even). There may be some clue for persons more learned than I; but

Shelley should have provided notes. Crashaw does not need *such* notes.

And when Shelley has some definite statement to make, he simply says it; keeps his images on one side and his meanings on the other:

> We look before and after,
>   And pine for what is not:
> Our sincerest laughter
>   With some pain is fraught;
> Our sweetest songs are those that tell of saddest thought.

This is a sweeping assertion, and is rather commonplace in expression; but it is intelligible. And it is not in the least like Crashaw.

I call Crashaw a 'devotional' poet, because the word 'religious' is so abused. Shelley even has been called religious, but he could not be called devout; he is religious in the same sense as when we say that Dean Inge or the Bishop of Birmingham is religious. Devotional poetry is religious poetry which falls within an exact faith and has precise objects for contemplation. Crashaw is sometimes called erotic in his devotion. 'Erotic' is an abused word, but in any case ought not to be an offensive word. In one aspect it may be applied to

Crashaw. Dante, for instance, always seems perfectly aware of every shade of both human and divine love; Beatrice is his means of transition between the two; and there is never any danger of his confounding the two loves. But just as Crashaw is deficient in humanity, and yet is neither quite in the world nor out of it, and so is neither a Dante nor an Adam of St. Victor, so we feel at times that his passion for heavenly objects is imperfect because it is partly a substitute for human passion. It is not impure, but it is incomplete.

Yet Crashaw is quite alone in his peculiar kind of greatness. He is alone among the metaphysical poets of England, who were mostly intensely English: Crashaw is primarily a European. He was saturated still more in Italian and Latin poetry than in English. Indeed Mr. Mario Praz, who has probably read more than anybody of the Latin poetry and the continental poetry of the seventeenth century, puts Crashaw above Marino, Góngora, and everybody else, merely as the *representative* of the baroque spirit in literature.

VIII

THE HUMANISM OF IRVING
BABBITT

I T is proverbially easier to destroy than to construct; and as a corollary of this proverb, it is easier for readers to apprehend the destructive than the constructive side of an author's thought. More than this: when a writer is skilful at destructive criticism, the public is satisfied with that. If he has no constructive philosophy, it is not demanded; and if he has, it is overlooked. This is especially true when we are concerned with critics of society, from Arnold to the present day. All such critics are criticized from one common standard, and that the lowest: the standard of brilliant attack upon aspects of contemporary society which we know and dislike. It is the easiest standard to take. For the criticism deals with concrete things in our world which we know, and the writer may be merely echoing, in neater phrasing, our own thoughts; whereas the construction deals with things hard and unfamiliar. Hence the popularity of Mr. Mencken.

But there are more serious critics than Mr. Mencken, and of these we must ask in the end what they have to offer in place of what they denounce. M. Julien Benda, for instance, makes it a part of his deliberate programme to offer nothing; he has a romantic view of critical detachment which limits his interest. Mr. Wyndham Lewis is obviously striving courageously toward a positive theory, but in his published work has not yet reached that point. But in Professor Babbitt's latest book, *Democracy and Leadership*, the criticism is related to a positive theory and dependent upon it. This theory is not altogether expounded, but is partly assumed. What I wish to do in the present essay is to ask a few questions of Mr. Babbitt's constructive theory.

The centre of Mr. Babbitt's philosophy is the doctrine of humanism. In his earlier books we were able to accept this idea without

analysis; but in *Democracy and Leadership*—
which I take to be at this point the summary
of his theory—we are tempted to question it.
The problem of humanism is undoubtedly
related to the problem of religion. Mr.
Babbitt makes it very clear, here and there
throughout the book, that he is unable to take
the religious view—that is to say that he cannot accept any dogma or revelation; and that
humanism is the *alternative* to religion. And
this brings up the question: is this alternative
any more than a *substitute*? and if a substitute,
does it not bear the same relation to religion
that 'humanitarianism' bears to humanism? Is
it, in the end, a view of life that will work by
itself, or is it a derivative of religion which
will work only for a short time in history,
and only for a few highly cultivated persons
like Mr. Babbitt—whose ancestral traditions,
furthermore, are Christian, and who is, like
many people, at the distance of a generation
or so from definite Christian belief? Is it, in
other words, durable beyond one or two
generations?

Mr. Babbitt says, of the 'representatives of
the humanitarian movement', that

they wish to live on the naturalistic level, and at the same time to enjoy the benefits that the past had hoped to achieve as a result of some humanistic or religious discipline.

The definition is admirable, but provokes us to ask whether, by altering a few words, we cannot arrive at the following statement about humanists:

they wish to live on the humanistic level, and at the same time to enjoy the benefits that the past had hoped to achieve as a result of some religious discipline.

If this transposition is justified, it means that the difference is only of one step: the humanitarian has suppressed the properly human, and is left with the animal; the humanist has suppressed the divine, and is left with a human element which may quickly descend again to the animal from which he has sought to raise it.

Mr. Babbitt is a stout upholder of tradition and continuity, and he knows, with all his immense and encyclopedic information, that the Christian religion is an essential part of the history of our race. Humanism and religion are thus, as historical facts, by no means parallel; humanism has been sporadic, but Christianity continuous. It is quite irrelevant to conjecture the possible development of the European races without Christianity—to imagine, that is, a tradition of humanism equivalent to the actual tradition of Christianity. For all we can say is that we should have been very different creatures, whether better or worse. Our problem being to form the future, we can only form it on the materials of the past; we must *use* our heredity, instead of denying it. The religious habits of the race are still very strong, in all places, at all times, and for all people. There is no humanistic habit: humanism is, I think, merely the state of mind of a few persons in a few places at a few times. To exist at all, it is dependent upon some other attitude, for it is essentially critical—I would even say parasitical. It has been, and can still be, of great value; but it will never provide showers of partridges or abundance of manna for the chosen peoples.

It is a little difficult to define humanism in Mr. Babbitt's terms, for he is very apt to line it up in battle order *with* religion *against* humanitarianism and naturalism; and what I am trying to do is to *contrast* it with religion. Mr. Babbitt is very apt to use phrases like

'tradition humanistic and religious' which suggest that you could say also 'tradition humanistic *or* religious'.   So I must make shift to
define humanism as I can from a few of the
examples that Mr. Babbitt seems to hold up
to us.

I should say that he regarded Confucius,
Buddha, Socrates, and Erasmus as humanists
(I do not know whether he would include
Montaigne).   It may surprise some to see
Confucius and Buddha, who are popularly
regarded as founders of religions, in this list.
But it is always the human reason, not the
revelation of the supernatural, upon which
Mr. Babbitt insists.   Confucius and Buddha
are not in the same boat, to begin with.   Mr.
Babbitt of course knows infinitely more about
both of these men than I do; but even people
who know even less about them than I do,
know that Confucianism endured by fitting
in with popular religion, and that Buddhism
endured by becoming as distinctly a *religion*
as Christianity—recognizing a dependence of
the human upon the divine.

And finally, the attitude of Socrates and that
of Erasmus toward the religion of their place

[131]

and time were very different from what I take to be the attitude of Professor Babbitt. How far Socrates believed, and whether his legendary request of the sacrifice of a cock was merely gentlemanly behaviour or even irony, we cannot tell; but the equivalent would be Professor Babbitt receiving extreme unction, and that I cannot at present conceive. But both Socrates and Erasmus were content to remain critics, and to leave the religious fabric untouched. So that I find Mr. Babbitt's humanism to be very different from that of any of the humanists above mentioned.

This is no small point, but the question is a difficult one. It is not at all that Mr. Babbitt has *misunderstood* any of these persons, or that he is not fully acquainted with the civilizations out of which they sprang. On the contrary, he knows all about them. It is rather, I think, that in his interest in the messages of individuals —messages conveyed in books—he has tended merely to neglect the conditions. The great men whom he holds up for our admiration and example are torn from their contexts of race, place, and time. And in consequence, Mr. Babbitt seems to me to tear himself from his own context. His humanism is really something quite different from that of his exemplars, but (to my mind) alarmingly like very liberal Protestant theology of the nineteenth century: it is, in fact, a product—a by-product—of Protestant theology in its last agonies.

I admit that all humanists—as humanists —have been individualists. As humanists, they have had nothing to offer to the mob. But they have usually left a place, not only for the mob, but (what is more important) for the mob part of the mind in themselves. Mr. Babbitt is too rigorous and conscientious a Protestant to do that: hence there seems to be a gap between his own individualism (and indeed intellectualism, beyond a certain point, must be individualistic) and his genuine desire to offer something which will be useful to the American nation primarily and to civilization itself. But the historical humanist, as I understand him, halts at a certain point and admits that the reason will go no farther, and that it cannot feed on honey and locusts.

Humanism is either an alternative to religion, or is ancillary to it. To my mind, it always flourishes most when religion has been strong; and if you find examples of humanism which are anti-religious, or at least in opposition to the religious faith of the place and time, then such humanism is purely destructive, for it has never found anything to replace what it destroyed. Any religion, of course, is for ever in danger of petrifaction into mere ritual and habit, though ritual and habit be essential to religion. It is only renewed and refreshed by an awakening of feeling and fresh devotion, or by the critical reason. The latter may be the part of the humanist. But if so, then the function of humanism, though necessary, is secondary. You cannot make humanism itself into a religion.

What Mr. Babbitt, on one side, seems to me to be trying to do is to make humanism—his own form of humanism—work without religion. For otherwise, I cannot see the significance of his doctrine of self-control. This doctrine runs throughout his work, and sometimes appears as the 'inner check'. It appears as an alternative to both political and religious anarchy. In the political form it is more easily acceptable. As forms of government become more democratic, as the outer restraints of kingship, aristocracy, and class disappear, so it becomes more and more necessary that the individual no longer controlled by authority or habitual respect should control himself. So far, the doctrine is obviously true and impregnable. But Mr. Babbitt seems to think also that the 'outer' restraints of an orthodox religion, as they weaken, can be supplied by the inner restraint of the individual over himself. If I have interpreted him correctly, he is thus trying to build a Catholic platform out of Protestant planks. By tradition an individualist, and jealous of the independence of individual thought, he is struggling to make something that will be valid for the nation, the race, the world.

The sum of a population of individuals, all ideally and efficiently checking and controlling themselves, will never make a whole. And if you distinguish so sharply between 'outer' and 'inner' checks as Mr. Babbitt does, then there is nothing left for the individual to check himself by but his own private notions and his judgment, which is pretty precarious. As a matter of fact, when you leave the political field for the theological, the distinction between outer and inner becomes far from clear. Given the most highly organized and temporally powerful hierarchy, with all the powers of inquisition and punishment imaginable, still the idea of the religion is the *inner* control— the appeal not to a man's behaviour but to his soul. If a religion cannot touch a man's self, so that in the end he is controlling himself instead of being merely controlled by priests as he might be by policemen, then it has failed in its professed task. I suspect Mr. Babbitt at times of an instinctive dread of organized religion, a dread that it should cramp and deform the free operations of his own mind. If so, he is surely under a misapprehension.

And what, one asks, are all these millions, even these thousands, or the remnant of a few intelligent hundreds, going to control themselves *for*? Mr. Babbitt's critical judgment is exceptionally sound, and there is hardly one of his several remarks that is not, by itself, acceptable. It is the joints of his edifice, not the materials, that sometimes seem a bit weak. He says truly:

[136]

It has been a constant experience of man in all ages that mere rationalism leaves him unsatisfied. Man craves in some sense or other of the word an enthusiasm that will lift him out of his merely rational self.

But it is not clear that Mr. Babbitt has any other enthusiasm to offer except the enthusiasm for being lifted out of one's merely rational self by some enthusiasm. Indeed, if he can infect people with enthusiasm for getting even up to the level of their rational selves, he will accomplish a good deal.

But this seems to me just the point at which 'humanistic control' ends, if it gets that far. He speaks of the basis 'of religion and humanistic control' in Burke, but what we should like to know is the respective parts played by religion and humanism in this basis. And with all the references that Mr. Babbitt makes to the rôle of religion in the past, and all the connexions that he perceives between the decline of theology and the growth of the modern errors that he detests, he reveals himself as uncompromisingly detached from any religious belief, even the most purely 'personal':

To be modern has meant practically to be increasingly positive and critical, to refuse to receive anything on an

[137]

authority 'anterior, exterior, and superior' to the individual.
With those who still cling to the principle of outer authority
I have no quarrel. I am not primarily concerned with them.
I am myself a thoroughgoing individualist, writing for those
who are, like myself, irrevocably committed to the modern
experiment. In fact, so far as I object to the moderns at all,
it is because they have not been sufficiently modern, or, what
amounts to the same thing, have not been sufficiently experi-
mental.

Those of us who lay no claim to being modern
may not be involved in the objection, but, as
bystanders, we may be allowed to inquire
where all this modernity and experimenting is
going to lead. Is everybody to spend his
time experimenting? And on what, and to
what end? And if the experimenting merely
leads to the conclusion that self-control is
good, that seems a very frosty termination
to our hunt for 'enthusiasm'. What is the
higher will to *will*, if there is nothing either
'anterior, exterior, or superior' to the individual?
If this will is to have anything on which to
operate, it must be in relation to external
objects and to objective values. Mr. Babbitt
says:

To give the first place to the higher will is only another
way of declaring that life is an act of faith. One may dis-

cover on positive grounds a deep meaning in the old Christian tenet that we do not know in order that we may believe, but we believe in order that we may know.

This is quite true; but if life is an act of faith, in what is it an act of faith? The Life-Forcers, with Mr. Bernard Shaw at their head, would say I suppose 'in Life itself'; but I should not accuse Mr. Babbitt of anything so silly as that. However, a few pages further on he gives something more definite to will: it is civilization.

The next idea, accordingly, to be examined is that of civilization. It seems, on the face of it, to mean something definite; it is in fact, merely a frame to be filled with definite objects, not a definite object itself. I do not believe that I can sit down for three minutes to will civilization without my mind's wandering to something else. I do not mean that civilization is a mere word; the word means something quite real. But the minds of the individuals who can be said to 'have willed civilization' are minds filled with a great variety of objects of will, according to place, time, and individual constitution; what they have in common is rather a habit in the same direction than a will to civilization. And unless by civilization you mean material progress, cleanliness, etc. —which is not what Mr. Babbitt means; if you mean a spiritual and intellectual co-ordination on a high level, then it is doubtful whether civilization can endure without religion, and religion without a church.

I am not here concerned with the question whether such a 'humanistic' civilization as that aimed at by Professor Babbitt is or is not *desirable*; only with the question whether it is *feasible*. From this point of view the danger of such theories is, I think, the danger of collapse. For those who had not followed Mr. Babbitt very far, or who had felt his influence more remotely, the collapse would be back again into humanitarianism thinly disguised. For others who had followed him hungrily to the end and had found no hay in the stable, the collapse might well be into a Catholicism *without* the element of humanism and criticism, which would be a Catholicism of despair. There is a hint of this in Mr. Babbitt's own words:

The choice to which the modern man will finally be reduced, it has been said, is that of being a Bolshevist or a

Jesuit. In that case (assuming that by Jesuit is meant the ultramontane Catholic) there does not seem to be much room for hesitation. Ultramontane Catholicism does not, like Bolshevism, strike at the very root of civilization. In fact, under certain conditions that are already partly in sight, the Catholic Church may perhaps be the only institution left in the Occident that can be counted upon to uphold civilized standards. It may also be possible, however, to be a thoroughgoing modern and at the same time civilized. . . .

The last sentence somehow seems to me to die away a little faintly. But the point is that Mr. Babbitt seems to be giving away to the Church in anticipation more than would many who are more concerned with it in the present than he. Mr. Babbitt is much more ultramontane than I am. One may feel a very deep respect and even love for the Catholic Church (by which I understand Mr. Babbitt means the hierarchy in communion with the Holy See); but if one studies its history and vicissitudes, its difficulties and problems past and present, one is struck with admiration and awe certainly, but is not the more tempted to place all the hopes of humanity on one institution.

But my purpose has been, not to predict a bad end for Mr. Babbitt's philosophy, but to

point out the direction which I think it should
follow if the obscurities of 'humanism' were
cleared up. It should lead, I think, to the
conclusion that the humanistic point of view
is auxiliary to and dependent upon the religious
point of view. For us, religion is of course
Christianity; and Christianity implies, I think,
the conception of the Church. It would be
not only interesting but invaluable if Professor
Babbitt, with his learning, his great ability,
his influence, and his interest in the most
important questions of the time, could reach
this point. His influence might thus join
with that of another philosopher of the same
rank—Charles Maurras—and might, indeed,
correct some of the extravagances of that
writer.

Such a consummation is impossible. Professor Babbitt knows too much; and by that
I do not mean merely erudition or information
or scholarship. I mean that he knows too
many religions and philosophies, has assimi-
lated their spirit too thoroughly (there is
probably no one in England or America who
understands early Buddhism better than he)
to be able to give himself to any. The result

is humanism. I believe that it is better to recognize the weaknesses of humanism at once, and allow for them, so that the structure may not crash beneath an excessive weight; and so that we may arrive at an enduring recognition of its value for us, and of our obligation to its author.